BEYOND THE BREAK

BEYOND
THE
BREAK

CHRISTO HALL

BEYOND THE BREAK

THE **SURF-INSPIRED SUCCESS CODE** FOR BUSINESS AND LIFE

WILEY

First published in 2024 by John Wiley & Sons Australia, Ltd
Level 4, 600 Bourke St, Melbourne, Victoria 3000, Australia

Typeset in Warnock Pro 11.5/16.5 pts

© John Wiley & Sons Australia, Ltd 2024

The moral rights of the author have been asserted

ISBN: 978-1-394-28083-4

 A catalogue record for this
book is available from the
National Library of Australia

Cover design by Wiley
Cover image: © Abstract Aerial Art/Getty Images
Back cover and internal photos: © Simon Anderson

Disclaimer

The material in this publication is of the nature of general comment only, and does not represent professional advice. It is not intended to provide specific guidance for particular circumstances and it should not be relied on as the basis for any decision to take action or not take action on any matter which it covers. Readers should obtain professional advice where appropriate, before making any such decision. To the maximum extent permitted by law, the author and publisher disclaim all responsibility and liability to any person, arising directly or indirectly from any person taking or not taking action based on the information in this publication.

CONTENTS

Introduction   *vii*

1   Hawaii   **1**
The biggest opportunities often appear to be mistakes

2   Narrabeen   **17**
*It's not about how hard you work; it's about the
results you get*

3   First European trip   **41**
The most powerful resource to generate success is you!

4   Australia   **61**
Know your purpose

5   Indonesia   **77**
Look where you want to go

6   Maldives   **91**
Routines are magic

7   Africa   **109**
I've already lost, so I have nothing to lose

8   France   **121**
Where your focus goes, results flow

9   Spain and Portugal   **139**
Done is better than perfect

10 **Kangaroo and Canary Islands**   **153**
    Your beliefs about yourself are BS
11 **Japan and Brazil**   **167**
    Invest in growth
12 **Hawaii and home (again)**   **181**
    Learn, have fun and maintain health

Going beyond the break   *203*

INTRODUCTION

From my late teens I was a professional surfer, and I spent seven amazing years travelling the world competing on the world surfing circuit. Casting my mind back over my adventurous (and wild) professional surfing days, and bringing you the stories I share in this book, enabled me to recognise a pattern. Recurring fears surfaced in almost a systematic way, event after event. They are so clear to me now, but early in my career, on a day-to-day basis, the destructive thoughts were inescapable and hard to distinguish. A negative thought here, a feeling of discomfort there. En masse, they were enough to cause me to doubt myself, to procrastinate instead of making a decision, and to tear down careful planning.

It's incredible to me now to see how I would move through the same phases of anxiety leading up to each big surfing event or life decision. My inner voice would prod, prompt and nudge me away from my pre-event routine, sometimes over a period of weeks. My anxious mind would pull out every trick in the book — from giving me dreams about trying and failing, running late for an event or not being able to find my surfboard, to reminding me about every mistake I'd ever made or chastising me for skipping a workout.

But I also noticed another, more powerful, pattern. Many of my happiest moments in life came right after doing something that pushed me well outside my comfort zone. Making a difficult decision, pushing through a challenge against fear and taking action was fulfilling.

What I also realise now is that my surfing career had *transferrable skills*. Of course, I had massive concerns about ending a sports career, and being in my late twenties with no qualifications. But I found myself drawing on my professional surfing experience, and began to understand this experience was comparable to a powerful qualification. I'd had different life experiences to most people, and these experiences made me more effective in business. They gave me a process to compete in any space. They prepared me for business success.

Nothing has been handed to me or accidentally fallen in my lap. I've worked hard for my successes and taken chances to get ahead, overcoming mental and physical challenges.

I learnt from my surfing career *not* to shy away from challenges, but to embrace them as a pathway to happiness. The secret to fulfilment seems to be discomfort — or, at least, the path that pushes through the unfamiliar leads to discomfort, which (eventually) leads to fulfilment. (We certainly are strange creatures.)

I've realised the same mental challenges I faced in surfing are faced by all of us every single day. Sometimes these challenges are obvious, due to a large change or eruption of events, but often these challenges are almost unrecognisable because they happen so fast, or seem insignificant in the moment, only to reveal themselves when the tide goes out. However, your approach to these challenges — large and seemingly insignificant — has a huge impact on your results, and my lessons from the ocean will show you how to overcome them.

I've used the competitive knowledge I gained from professional surfing to build multiple successful businesses, and mentor others to generate hundreds of millions in additional revenue. All over the world and across many different types of media, I've been asked to share my unique approach to business — when in my mind, all I'm doing is surfing.

In *Beyond the Break* I do more than share my stories from seven years competing on the world surfing tour. I also give you strategies that can be applied to succeed in business, a career, sports or any hobby.

I provide insights into how to handle, and sometimes work with, your inner critic. (I've even given mine a name — introducing Bronco, everybody.) Similar to watching a set come in and picking the right wave to surf all the way to shore, I help you understand your limits, pick your battles and overcome failure. If you get dumped, you can dust yourself off, maybe spit out a mouthful of sand, learn your lessons and move on.

Most importantly, in this book I help you hone your mindset and find your true motivation — so you can carve through even the choppiest of seas.

So what are you waiting for? Grab your board, and let's go.

CHAPTER 1

HAWAII

The biggest opportunities often appear to be mistakes

The oppressive humidity was the first thing that hit me when I stepped through the doors of the Hawaii International Airport, weary after a nine-hour haul from Sydney. On the plane I'd been barely able to keep my eyes open, but now I was hyped on expectation. World surfing circuit here I come. I had been anxious for months, knowing that Hawaii, with its life-threatening powerful waves, was the ultimate testing ground for an up-and-coming professional surfer.

Beads of sweat gathered in my hairline as I dragged a suitcase and huge board bag off the walkway and set them down.

Keenan dumped his gear beside mine. 'Well, we're not in Narrabeen anymore. What time's our ride supposed to be here, Christo?'

I pulled a printed page from a pocket of my board shorts and unfolded it. Our flight itinerary and some details I had scribbled under it were all I had. 'It's five past midnight, so we landed a little early. The sponsor guy back home said a photographer they're using would pick us up. Should be here any minute.'

Several of the passengers glanced quizzically at us as they scurried towards hire cars and taxis. No doubt they were wondering where our parents were. I smiled to myself. Nope, this sixteen year old was going to take the world by storm single-handedly.

Hawaii was a mystery to me, other than what I knew from the televised world surfing competitions I'd watched over the years. The island had been shrouded in darkness as we landed and the bright fluorescent lighting of the airport looked pretty much like any other cement monstrosity, but it wouldn't be long before we were on the beach, in the waves.

In the time it took me to down the last of the water I had in a plastic bottle, all the other passengers had cleared out. Keenan opened his board bag and checked that none of his seven boards had been damaged in transit. Stress head.

I raised a chin in question.

'All good,' he confirmed.

Ten minutes later, the lights went out at all the rental car stations. My gut twisted a little. Best laid plans and all...

Keenan rubbed the back of his neck, pacing the empty forecourt.

'Maybe he's running late,' I offered. Orange light glowed above a public phone box. 'I haven't got a number for him, but we could phone the sponsor guy. You got coins?'

Keenan fished in his wallet and shook his head, showing me his palm with a few Australian coins on it. Not helpful.

The click of a deadbolt sliding into place sounded behind me. Keenan's eyes widened and we glanced at one another. The airport forecourt was quiet, lights going out inside the terminal. Even the taxi rank was empty. A lone stretch limousine driver paced the pavement as he finished up a smoke. We made eye contact and he nodded.

'You two need a ride?' he called, dropping the cigarette to the ground and twisting the ball of his foot on it.

'I guess so. How much?' I eyed the glossy, black vehicle that looked way out of our budget.

'Where are you headed?'

I looked at Keenan, who shrugged. The sponsor had organised all that stuff, supposedly.

'Um, North Shore.' That's all I could remember.

The driver frowned. 'That's a big area. Can you narrow it down?'

I shot Keenan a pleading look.

'It's near Rocky Point?' he suggested. 'I reckon he said the accommodation was just to the left of the Rocky Point beach track.'

Well, that would have to do for now.

'It's on my way home,' the driver said, 'so I'll do it for a hundred dollars. Are you meeting your family?'

'No, we're here to surf.' I stood tall and thrust my chest forward a little, proud.

'No kidding?' The driver helped store our luggage, the limousine so long our board bags fitted in the back with us. 'Wow, you'll get to surf the best waves in the world here, but beware — the waves here are also the most dangerous in the world.'

'We sure hope we get some good ones.' I handed over fifty US dollars and so did Keenan. It was all we had in our wallets but it wasn't like we had any other option.

Less than an hour later we had arrived at Rocky Point, and were standing on the footpath in the dark, luggage at our feet.

'You sure you boys will be all right on your own?' The limo driver looked doubtful.

'No worries.' I flashed him a smile full of confidence I didn't feel.

Palm leaves swayed overhead, dark silhouettes against a purple sky, as the limousine pulled away. The sound of rolling waves thundered nearby.

'What now?' Keenan tapped a foot, manically searching the empty street for answers.

He was a year older, so I left the worrying to him and figured out a solution.

I glanced at my watch: 3.30 am. 'I need to crash, man. Let's hit the beach and see if we can find our accommodation when it's light.'

We tentatively made our way down a narrow track towards the beach, the moonlight so weak I could barely see a metre in front of me. The sand that trickled over and under my thong-clad feet was icy cold and dense bushes crowded the pathway, but the familiarity of the salt-laden air beckoned me forwards.

At the top of the beach, the power of the waves reverberated through the night air, filling me with excitement and apprehension in equal measure. I could just make out white water in the shallows and black nothingness beyond.

We laid our bags on the soft sand at the top of the beach and lay down, a jumper rolled up for a pillow, a hand and foot touching each piece of luggage for security. My new Billabong hoodie provided minimal insulation from the sand and I curled into a ball to minimise the shivering.

Sleep came in fits, plagued by images of monster waves crushing me and waking to find my belongings stolen.

◆ ◆ ◆

I woke with a start, hands grabbing for my luggage. Still where I left it.

Then I sprang to my feet, spitting sand from my mouth. Flicking my hands systematically through my hair and down my body, I dusted off the sand coating one side of me. A light breeze had picked up and I shivered, cold through to the bone. I prodded Keenan with one foot.

'Screw this,' I said. 'I'm going to knock on doors until we find our accommodation. The sponsor said it was to the left of the Rocky Point track, right?'

Keenan nodded, rubbing sleepy eyes. 'It's still the middle of the night.' He shivered. 'But, okay. Let's do this.'

I grabbed my luggage and dragged the lot back up the track, Keenan hustling to follow.

Standing on the quiet road, I looked at the houses on either side of the track. Was it left when facing the beach, or left when coming up from the beach?

'This one's got boards outside,' Keenan stage-whispered, a sudden look of confidence in his eye.

Between the leaves of a lush garden, the faint glow of a lamp beckoned through a bare window. It was the only sign of life in the vicinity, so we crept towards the door.

The moment of truth was upon us as we stood like voyeurs on the dark porch, daring one another to intrude on a stranger in the middle of the night, but I was never one to back down in the face of a challenge. I took a deep breath, steeled myself and knocked forcefully. No going back now. Despite my show of bravery, I felt the urge to step back behind Keenan.

I was never one to back down in the face of a challenge.

We both flinched in the direction of the road, as though we might make a run for it. Then we heard it. Movement inside. Someone shuffled towards us. The door handle turned and I took a step back from the big, muscular French-Polynesian frowning down at me.

Square jaw, wide forehead, low-set brows…I knew this guy. 'Vetea David? No way.'

Oh hell, he was definitely going to pummel us for banging on his door in the middle of the night.

The big Tahitian's face softened and pearly whites flashed. 'You two lost?'

'Sorry for waking you, mate,' Keenan said. 'We're here to surf from Australia, but our ride didn't show up at the airport and we're not sure exactly where our accommodation is. It's somewhere around here. We both ride for Gorilla Grip.' Genius move by Keenan, I thought, to find something in common by mentioning Gorilla Grip, knowing that Vetea was also a team rider.

'Hey, no worries. I went to bed early and was up. Call me Poto. I'm hitting the waves shortly if you wanna bring your stuff in and come along.'

Shortly? It was still dark. Keenan shrugged at me.

'Thanks, that'd be cool,' I said.

We hurried to grab our gear.

Keenan whispered, 'We're hanging out with bloody Vetea David!'

I just grinned, taking it as a good sign. The surfing gods were finally favouring us today.

Some kind of jungle dance music was playing on the stereo, and it lent a surreal atmosphere to sitting at a melamine kitchen table while one of the big names in surfing rolled a fat smoke. He puffed away, while recapping the previous day's events at the Pipe Masters competition. This comp was the pinnacle of world surfing events, and pretty soon I'd be riding the world-famous Pipeline break too.

'Where you boys say you were from?'

'We flew in from Australia at midnight,' I told him, 'and some photographer was supposed to pick us up.'

'Oh, hell. There's a photographer dude staying here,' Poto said, 'and he mentioned something about picking a couple of teenagers up. Man, he went to a strip club earlier, to kill some time. Ha ha.'

A least someone was having fun. I was knackered from the long flight and shivering on the beach. My body screamed for sleep, but my mind was racing. This was the big league and I was on my way to surfing the greatest waves on Earth with the world's top surfers.

Poto sucked the last of his smoke and ground out the butt in an ashtray. 'Let's go surfing.'

I glanced out the window. Still dark. *This is it, Christo. Surfing Pipeline in the dark. I guess this is how you die.* I forced the nagging voice out of my head. This is what I came here for; to ride monster waves.

'How big do you think the waves will be?' I asked nervously, opening my board bag.

'It's gonna be big. Take your biggest board. Yesterday, it was a ten-foot Hawaiian swell.'

Keenan pulled a board from his bag. 'Hawaiian?'

Poto laughed, a rich, melodic sound. 'When they say ten-foot here, it's more like fifteen to twenty.'

'Holy shit.' My gut dropped. I sized up my suddenly insignificant seven-foot, six-inch board against Poto's massive board.

'The way surfers measure wave height must be the eighth wonder of the world, bro. Or maybe the early surfers were too stoned to judge.' Poto laughed heartily.

'Or maybe they had enormous balls.'

'Yeah,' Keenan piped in. 'I've said it's only eight foot out there when everyone else was saying it was ten, just to sound more hard core.'

'Well, it's much worse in Hawaii, bro.' Poto clapped me on the back. 'Big boys with big balls riding massive waves. They'll say it's a small swell when they're riding neck-breakers.'

'So, how big are you expecting the waves to be this morning?' I tried to sound offhand, as though it wasn't an issue for me.

'Big.' Was all Poto said.

Shit. He rides massive waves every other day and he's calling today's swell big…I gulp down a frisson of panic. Sure, I'd ridden a six-foot, eight-inch board before, but I'd hoped to ease into the bigger waves and new bigger equipment. Clearly Poto was more of a baptism by fire kind of guy.

We loaded the boards into Poto's rental car and five minutes later arrived at Ehukai Beach, home to the surf break known as Pipeline.

The thunder of monstrous waves smashing onto the shallow volcanic reef filled the still night air. My heart skipped a beat. It wasn't just the sound; I could *feel* the power of the waves vibrating underfoot. I glanced at Keenan, who widened his eyes in a silent communication of unease. I'd never planned on riding my first big wave in the dark but I was a pro surfer now. Despite my instincts telling me to stop, I was going to stare these monsters in the eye and make this happen — even if I couldn't see them.

I slung my board under one arm and followed Poto down a dirt track, into the darkness.

The houses either side of the beach access were being shook at their foundations by the deep rumble of the crashing waves.

> **I was going to stare these monsters in the eye and make this happen.**

Seaspray floated through the air and coated my skin, and the familiar taste of it on my tongue drew me closer. Thank goodness for an unimpeded moon, which cast just enough light that I could see where to place each foot.

We emerged on the beach, eyes searching for the waves but only able to glimpse white water in the shallows. Waves were right in front of me — almost close enough to reach out and touch — and yet I was faced with the black hole of a dragon's mouth. A rumble built in its belly to become a roar that rushed at me, tingling through my hands and feet, exhaling salty mist in my face. It was a force to be reckoned with.

Pipeline is one of the scariest breaks on Earth, completely different to anything I had ever ridden before. And here I was, getting ready to ride it. In the dark.

When I'd visualised surfing Pipeline, I had imagined sunshine, sparkling tropical warm water, palm trees and perfect waves. It was surreal to be waxing up my board now on the beach, beside one of the greatest surfers in the world, barely able to make out his silhouette.

'Let's go.' Poto stood, muscles tensed, expression serious. ''Ia mānuia.'

I stood behind him, game face on. 'Huh?'

'Good luck.' The white of teeth flashed and then he was running into the water.

'Let's do this,' I said to myself, and charged into the gaping mouth of the dragon.

I paddled swiftly, trying to stay close to Poto so I knew I was in the right place. Keenan was hot on my tail. The rhythmic strokes and cool water moving over me was soothing. This was where I loved to be.

We made our way through the waves as the first bruise of dawn backlit distant clouds. It was just enough to reveal the size of the waves breaking out the back. Big didn't cover it.

At first, I stayed wide, watching from a safe place where the waves weren't breaking. Reading the ocean. Feeling the ebb and flow of its power. Getting an understanding for the number of waves in a set and where the biggest ones broke.

I had enough light now to watch Poto catch a couple of waves, and I cut my teeth on a couple of smaller waves. Adrenaline kicked in and flowed through my limbs as I pushed the board over the crest of some giant waves.

By the time I worked up the courage to position myself for a bigger wave, around twenty other surfers were sitting out the back. It was more crowded than I was used to back in my home beach at Narrabeen first thing in the morning. Wave after wave, a bigger, more aggressive surfer slipped in front of me. Unless I was willing to go toe to toe with one of the locals, I might not get another ride.

Then, the planets aligned. A huge swell lifted in front of me. It was now or never. I glanced at a local sitting next to me, almost asking permission, and he looked me straight in the eyes and said, 'Go for it.' My heart sank with the reality of what I now had to do, but my instincts kicked in. No way was I missing a good wave — and at Pipeline no less.

I paddled hard towards the direction of the beach just as an older local started to paddle for the same wave. He was further out than me but pulled the water through saucer-sized hands in a hurry. This was turning into situation.

No, I wasn't going to miss this wave. I paddled faster, shoulders burning with the effort, mere seconds away from the point of no return. After that, the only way to get out of the local's way would be to throw myself off the board and submit to being thrashed by the full brunt of the wave.

The wave continued to build, lifting me closer to vertical with a twelve-foot drop below me. Just as the moment of truth arrived, the local stopped paddling, fading off the back of the wave and out of my line of sight. It was all mine.

After that, everything happened so fast I didn't have time to think. I operated on autopilot, letting the muscle memory of thousands of other waves guide my instincts. The ocean dropped away in front of me, taking my stomach with it. As the wave face became so vertical that I was about to fall, I leapt to my feet and mustered every bit of experience, strength and skill I possessed as I free-fell the height of a two-storey building. Hanging onto the board with the tips of my toes. Down, down, down.

The steep wall of water seemed never-ending, only the edge of my board clinging precariously to its vertical face. At the instant it started to barrel over me, I angled across the wave and, suddenly, I was inside the tube.

It was like time slowed. Immersed in the thrill of being at one with the untameable ocean, raw energy surrounding me, I crouched inside the spacious barrel of inky water. It was a glorious moment in time. I was flying through the tube, dragging the tips of my fingers through the water, perfectly positioned on a monster wave. At Pipeline.

I might even make it out of this alive.

A dazzling flash lit the inside of the tube as I raced past a photographer swimming through the wave. Then I flew out the end of the barrel, going faster than I ever had before and still on my feet. I couldn't help but grin.

Wanting to savour every last minute of this momentous occasion, I rode the wave far longer than I needed to — partly making sure I was clear of any waves coming from behind and partly because I needed a moment to myself. I stayed on that wave until there was hardly anything left, and then finally turned off the back and sank onto the board in total awe of what I'd just done.

With no other surfers nearby, I lay back on the board, staring up at the golden glow of dawn. Hell, after years of watching movies and reading articles in magazines about Pipeline, I had really done it. I had ridden a monster wave and survived.

Adrenaline was still surging through my body, heart pounding my ribs, and then my legs started buzzing, kneecaps shaking uncontrollably. I shook out my legs, but it didn't relax them so I just lay there and

> **I had ridden a monster wave and survived.**

breathed while hiding my shaking knees under the water. As I took deep, satisfied breaths, a surge of confidence came over me. Maybe I was ready to face the journey ahead. To become a success. To become a man.

An overwhelming feeling of being exactly where I was supposed to be flooded through me. I loved the unpredictability of the ocean. It could be unforgiving, cruel even, but for those of us who dared to brave it, to play with the danger, it provided proof that dreams could come true.

Lessons from the ocean
The biggest opportunities often appear to be mistakes

Sometimes the biggest opportunities appear at first glance to be the worst potential mistakes, or the silliest things you could do (like riding Pipeline in the dark). But it's often these things that drive success and leave you feeling the most fulfilled. Sometimes you need to go against the grain and ignore what other people think, or at least what you imagine they might think.

I've built my business, Basic Bananas, to become Australia's largest marketing mentoring organisation for business owners. When I first started it, however, I had a business advisor who was very successful herself. She said the name 'Basic Bananas' was a big mistake and instead advised that my business should be called something along the lines of 'Million Dollar Marketing', 'Small Business Marketing Australia', or 'Your Marketing Guru'. None of these names sat well with me or my business partner—they were too dry, cheesy and non-memorable. We wanted to relate to small businesspeople who could have a bit of fun while being successful. So, against her advice and some personal fears, we named the business Basic Bananas.

To my surprise, only 18 months later I heard that same business advisor sharing in a presentation why Basic Bananas was such an amazing example of great branding.

Carve your path

◆ Take a minute now to think back to a time in business,
your career or your personal life when you felt really
fulfilled. Try to think of seemingly small things—the kind
of things you can implement again. If you visited Paris
and felt fulfilled, that's awesome, but it might be hard
to do every weekend. Maybe it was a big change you
made or maybe it was a small thing you implemented.
It could be something as simple as dedicating time
and committing to doing a task you had previously
been procrastinating about, or learning something new.
Stretch yourself to think of something you can do again
in the not-too-distant future.

◆ Think deeply about what you did that led to this feeling
of being fulfilled. Did you ignore external pressure, or
maybe perceived external pressure, going against the
opinion of others to follow your gut?

◆ Once you have more of an idea of the actions that led to
your feelings of fulfilment, practise replicating, or at least
schedule to replicate (if possible) those same actions!
Can you manufacture the same kind of situation again,
or can you do something new to push your business,
career, health or otherwise to a new level of satisfaction?

CHAPTER 2

NARRABEEN

It's not about how hard you work; it's about the results you get

After the thrills of my first surfing trip to Hawaii and riding the famous Pipeline, let me backtrack a little... okay, all the way back to my childhood.

In the mid-1980s, Narrabeen in northern Sydney hadn't yet flourished into the affluent Sydney suburb it is now. Back then, it had an unassuming, village-like feel to it, with a mixture of traditional brick homes and weatherboard shacks nestled among coastal scrub and pines. Pelicans and ducks ruled the lagoon that flowed to the sea. Most neighbours knew one another, and children roamed the streets. I suppose growing up a stone's throw from the beach predisposed me to a meaningful relationship with the ocean. I rode my first wave at the age of six and from then on, it was all I wanted to do. I drew waves in my school books, surfed every chance I got and, when that wasn't possible, pretended I was surfing the streets of Narrabeen on my skateboard.

I'll never forget that first glorious glide into shore. My two older brothers, Nick and Alex, and I had all been given bright yellow boogie boards for Christmas, and we barely waited for lunch to digest before heading to the beach to test them out.

Nick and Alex were familiar with the ocean, but Dad swam out with me, gently lifting me over the breaking waves as I clutched tightly to my new board.

'Paddle,' Dad commanded as a wave approached.

Just as the rising water caught me, Dad gave me a shove forwards.

The front of the boogie board angled high out of the water and suddenly I was on the wave, its momentum carrying me towards the beach. I had never felt such speed or power. Like I was flying!

With a white-knuckled grip on the front of the board, I raised one hand and thrust a fist in front of me, like superman leading the way. That was it. I was hooked — and I have never been able to get enough of the ocean since.

Between the beach and the lagoon, I was constantly in the water, always struggling to keep up with Nick and Alex. The Narrabeen Lagoon was right outside our door, and its still waters were the perfect place to amuse ourselves without needing parental supervision.

We created games using whatever we could get our hands on, such as the neighbour's old canoe or random windsurfers that washed up after a storm (the boards and sails, not the people). But a particular favourite was a tiny little fibreglass paddle boat we found. It would have barely fit two adults, but as kids we'd all pile into it. After paddling it into the middle of the lagoon, we'd slide to opposite sides and start to rock. Up and down, up and down. When water sloshed over the sides, we only rocked it harder, until it flipped and sunk. Of course, the whole endeavour of retrieving it and dragging it back to shore was equally fun. It was a game we played over and over again.

My big brother Alex had an incredible blue surfboard that, to my young eyes, looked like a magical device that could transport you to another dimension. I sensed its value was way beyond my years to comprehend, and could only imagine what it was *actually* designed for.

Sometimes, when Alex wasn't home I would carefully lug the heavy board down to the lagoon and paddle around on it. It was huge in comparison to my six-year-old body and, when I stood on it, it felt like a floating pontoon. If I was lucky enough to snag a really windy day, I'd try to stand on the board and catch the choppy waves, which would usually just throw me off.

◆ ◆ ◆

When I finally got my own 'board', it was a floppy piece of blue foam, which I called Foamy, with a channel running underneath it from nose to tail in lieu of a fin, to keep it travelling in a straight line.

I took Foamy on a family camping trip to Seal Rocks Beach when I was seven. The sand was pristine white, sun shimmered invitingly on the clear, turquoise water and I was eager to catch up to my brothers, who surfed the small waves by themselves.

Dad didn't ride a surfboard, but he always swam out with me and bodysurfed back to the beach. I was soon paddling out past the breaking waves to where my brothers were, and I watched them catch waves until, finally, I was bold enough to give it a try myself.

With my back to the waves, gaze intensely focused on where I wanted to be, I learnt an important lesson about the changeability of the ocean. A large wave crashed over me, tearing me from Foamy, pinning me underwater and tumbling my scrawny body like a ragdoll in a washing machine. Perhaps it was the years already spent in the water, sinking boats and chasing brothers, but I wasn't afraid. Indeed, there wasn't time for that as I held onto the last gasp of air in my lungs and waited for the wave to push me into the shallows.

At last, I figured out which way was up and clawed for the surface, breaking through, mouth open and gasping. A strong hand lifted me under one arm and I stood in the shallows, blinking up into Dad's horrified expression. Okay, maybe I should have been a little afraid, but there was a certain thrill to surviving something that scared even Dad. I puffed out my chest and grinned.

> **There was a certain thrill to surviving something that scared even Dad.**

'That'll teach you to always keep one eye on the incoming waves,' Alex called.

Foamy washed ashore, no worse for wear. I glared at the unpredictable ocean, picturing myself standing on my board, riding a wave all the way to shore. No way was one dumping going to scare me out of the water. So I paddled right back out.

As I was battling to get through the breaking waves, Nick caught a wave right in front of me. He jumped to his feet, turned his board parallel to the beach and rode across the green, unbroken face of the wave. The world went silent as I watched, open-mouthed. Man and board were one, streaking across the smooth face of the unbroken wave. It was something I'd only ever seen in pictures before, but here was my brother, gliding perfectly across the water like some kind of surf god.

That was all I wanted to do.

Again and again I wiped out that weekend but I never gave up trying. I was rewarded occasionally by being upright on the board for a few seconds at a time. It was enough. No matter what I had to do, I was going to surf like my brothers on a real board … one day soon.

On the way home from this camping trip, Foamy flew off the roof of the car, never to be seen again. I needed a new board. A real board. But for that, I would need money.

By the time Christmas rolled around, I had saved eighty dollars and Mum came through by giving me another fifty. At the time, one hundred and thirty dollars was an unimaginably large amount for an eight year old!

Alex took me to the local surf shop, chatting boisterously about how to pick a good board. I kept a hand clamped protectively over my pocket, scanning the street for robbers. The surf shop was the coolest place on Earth to me, and I was here with my big brother, a world-savvy fourteen year old who knew his way around surfing gear. He also knew Mike, the shop owner, who guided us towards his cheapest boards.

'Alex could help you fix one up,' he suggested.

'No, I want a really good board. I've got a hundred and thirty dollars.' I held the crumpled notes out on the palm of my hand.

I looked towards the racks of gorgeous, fibreglass boards adorned with tropical flowers, artistic flames and modern patterns, all in the colours of summer. Then I moved closer and flipped a few price tags over. *Gulp.* They were all several hundred dollars. My heart sunk into the pit of my stomach.

'I've got some great second-hand boards,' Mike said, pointing towards a rack that wasn't quite as shabby as the cheap ones or quite as shiny as the new ones.

An entrepreneur is born

My brothers spent their pocket and birthday money the second they received it, but it had always been in my nature to plan for the future. Mum even boasted to her friends, 'He's such a good little saver.' I still have the very first bank account she helped me set up as a child.

So, I had always saved, but once I realised I needed a proper surfboard, I had a purpose. And that's when my entrepreneurial side surfaced.

The surf shop shelf

My first enterprise was Christo's Surf Shop. I bought stickers and trinkets at the local surf shop with my one- and two-cent coins, cleared a shelf in my bedroom and invited friends to shop. No-one ever did. I suppose that was my first insight into the true nature of running a business (according to *Entrepreneur* magazine, 30 per cent fail by the end of the second year). Even though I never made a sale, I loved having some surfy things on display in my room.

The lolly initiative

My next business hit on the importance of demand, and what could be more desirable to children than lollies? The school I attended didn't allow lollies in the canteen, so I used my pocket money to buy some at the local shop before boarding the school bus. I then sold them at lunchtime to other students—for a profit, of course. I sold out my first day, so the next day I invested my earnings into a new batch of stock.

I soon made a name for myself in the schoolyard because the lollies had their own inbuilt marketing—they turned your mouth and lips blue. Other kids noticed blue lips and asked where they could get a lolly too. Boom! More customers and sales for me.

Pretty soon, children rushed me first thing in the morning so they wouldn't miss out, and I sold all of my stock every day. It was so profitable that I could afford to keep a few lollies to give to friends and enjoy some myself while still taking a profit. It was the perfect business...for a while.

This tiny business gave me valuable insights into focusing on and selling only my most popular products to save me time and make the most money. I tried a few other products to expand my range, but realised the blue lollies were the most popular and generated the highest profit, so all other products were swiftly cut. This lesson continues to serve me to this day—just focus on what makes the most money in the least amount of time, and scale that up.

With all the blue mouths in the schoolyard, I guess it was inevitable that teachers were going to notice. One morning I got called into the principal's office and was told, in no uncertain terms, to shut the business down.

The 'I'll do anything'

When I turned eight, I hatched a more ambitious plan. I'd been saving for a new surfboard since our trip to Seal Rocks Beach. Now I decided I needed a real surfboard, made of

(continued)

fibreglass, like the boards my two older brothers rode, and I was determined to get one. For that, I needed more money.

I pestered anyone for any chore they would pay me for, including any housework and gardening, and even washing cars. I squirrelled away a few coins here and there. When Mum realised I was serious, she announced that for Christmas she would pitch in the difference to buy me a real surfboard.

The 'Can I offer you a seat, sir?'

My next business started by accident when the world surfing tour had an event at North Narrabeen Beach. On the way to watch the competition, I snuck down the alleyway behind a cafe and grabbed two discarded milk crates from a pile of them—one each for my friend and me to sit on while watching the surfing event from the beach.

'Hey, where'd you get the crate from, kid?' another spectator asked. 'I'll buy it off you for two dollars.'

Sold. Then I offered his friend my mate's crate for another two dollars.

The beach was crowded with spectators sitting on hot sand, so over the next few days, I grabbed more unwanted crates from behind the cafe, brought them to the beach and sold them. I made enough money to save some and indulge in the awesome chocolate thick shakes at the same cafe.

On the final day of the competition, I haggled with one guy over the price of my last crate.

'It's four dollars,' I told him.

'I'll give you one,' he bargained.

'No sale.' I took a step away, watching his reaction.

He scowled and when he realised I was walking away he upped his offer to three dollars and we had a deal. 'You're quite the entrepreneur, aren't you?' he said.

I had no idea what that word meant, but I stuck to my guns and felt like I got a fair price.

'How about this five-foot-two Aloha? It's in reasonable condition.' He lifted the board from the rack and placed it on the carpet for my inspection.

There were wear marks around the edges, but it was long and sleek and white, with a Mango board shorts logo underneath the fiberglass surface and three proper fins. Yes, I could glide across the waves on this.

'It's perfect!'

Walking home with my new board under one arm, my feet barely touched the ground. I said 'Hello' and waved to neighbours I'd barely spoken to before, flipping the board over to show my favourite side. Somehow it seemed my senses were keener; I could feel every blade of dry summer grass under my bare feet and smell the delicious melon scent of the wax on the deck of the board. I inhaled that scent as deeply as I could. It was the smell of *my* board.

That first board lived in my bedroom from then on, far too precious to be outside with my brothers' boards.

◆ ◆ ◆

The surfing scene at my home beach felt like the centre of the universe, with lots of up-and-coming professional surfers and surf brands present in the area. Narrabeen local Damien Hardman won the world surfing title in 1987 and went on to win again in 1991. Another local, Simon Anderson, had invented the three-fin Thruster design in 1981, regarded as the most significant innovation in the history of the sport and still used by most surfers and professionals to this day.

As I've mentioned, each year, one of the world surfing tour competitions was held at North Narrabeen Beach and attracted a large Sydney crowd.

Without fail, I would arrive at the beach early (with or without milk crates to sell). I'd get there before my friends, before the spectators, and watch the competitors prepare. They looked so calm, waxing their boards, chatting with fellow competitors, and eyeing the ocean with an expectant desire I was already familiar with.

I remained on the beach all day, barely eating in case I missed something. My mates would come and go but they couldn't lure me away. This right here was the ultimate fun.

The longer I watched, though, the more I realised it was fun for me and the crowd, but a job for the pro surfers. I chewed on that for a while. The competitors seemed like gods to me. Many of them adorned my bedroom walls, larger than life on posters. They made money surfing for a living! That got me thinking about surfing in a more serious light, as I imagined myself on the world tour, with announcers reading out my scores and spectators cheering my name.

By the age of ten, I was on the water almost every day. There was almost always someone to go surf with — if not my brothers, then a community of buddies who rode pushbikes to the beach with boards under our arms. I didn't mind that mine was a girls' bike — rebuilt by a mate's father — because the middle bar on girls' bikes are lower, which made it easier to get on and off with the board under one arm. It was all about the boards. On the odd occasion when no-one else was free to surf, I'd head out alone.

Most days I had no idea what the sea conditions would be, but it didn't deter me. I was pulled to the ocean like tides to the moon. When confronted with stormy weather and choppy seas, I would only venture halfway out, catching reforming waves close to shore.

But competitiveness seemed ingrained into all the males I knew, and sometimes drove us to do stupid things. One stormy afternoon, my friend Ben and I arrived at the beach to angry waves exploding as they broke. They pounded the beach with enough ferocity to whip up high piles of foam on the shore.

I had a sinking feeling in my belly. The physical pain of being kept from something I loved.

We sat, watching the messy waves with glum expressions for a while. Then I turned to Ben. His gaze searched the white water, resting on a calmer channel near the rock pool.

'It's dangerous,' I said.

Ben nodded. 'A rip.'

Below the calmer surface lurked a strong current moving all that angry water out to the main break and the deep sea.

'We wouldn't have to go out to the main break, though.' That was where the biggest waves were. 'We could just paddle out a bit.'

'Stick to the channel where the waves aren't as powerful,' Ben agreed, warming to the idea.

I shrugged. 'We rode all the way down here.' I glanced along the beach. Not another soul. This was insane.

'Let's do it.'

As I waded through the foam, my muscles twitched from the adrenaline surging through them, ready for the onslaught. Neither of us said a word as we paddled to our possible doom. No way would I do something this stupid if I was on my own but I wasn't going to let Ben show me up either.

We caught a few of the smaller waves, checking in on one another often. If I held up a finger to signal 'one last wave' or pointed towards the beach, I'm sure Ben would have been relieved. But I didn't. I couldn't be the first to give in.

After a few manageable waves in the channel, a larger set came in, building and building until it towered over me. For a fleeting moment, I felt the backward pull of the wave and paddled like hell to catch it. Not quick enough, I missed catching the wave properly, so tried to stop and let it pass under me, but I was too late to pull out. The power of the wave pulled me forward with it as it broke, throwing me towards the beach, ripping the board from my grasp and tossing me around underwater.

I resurfaced, spluttering and waiting for the surf to push me back towards the shore. But the rip had me in its grasp now, and an invisible iron fist was dragging me away from the beach towards the bigger waves at the back. Wide-eyed, I searched for Ben, but there was no sign of him in the cold, grey ocean. My heart thrashed desperately. This had been a mistake.

And then I caught a glimpse of Ben's blonde head bobbing further out. He was paddling frantically for the beach, while being sucked deeper out to sea.

My limbs were shaking with fear, lungs burning from exertion, so I went against every instinct in my body and stopped fighting the rip. My brothers had both told me that you can't fight a rip. 'Go with it and paddle to the edge,' they said. This was perhaps my first understanding that the obvious route wasn't always the one that worked. Work with the current rather than fight it.

I signalled to Ben to paddle sideways out of the rip, and he gave me a shaky thumbs up, followed by one finger. He wanted only one more wave. It didn't matter what wave I caught, anything that took me to shore would do. Once we were out of the rip, a big wave carried us into the churning shallows, where we hauled ourselves onto the sand and sat next to our boards, breathing heavily.

The obvious route wasn't always the one that worked. Work with the current rather than fight it.

I've retold the tale of this misadventure many times with bravado, but in reality I was really scared and never underestimated the power of the ocean again.

◆ ◆ ◆

That tiny kernel of belief that I might someday attain fame and fortune, hatched while watching the world tour event, spurred my competitiveness into overdrive — with myself, my friends and the ocean. So, when Nick and a few of his friends decided to set up a surf competition for me and my friends, I couldn't say no.

It was a sweltering summer's day and the beach was lined with bathers, umbrellas and towels. Children squealed in the shallows, a dog chased seagulls along the shoreline and the ocean glistened like a jewel.

'We'll judge and you guys compete.' Nick split us into two groups and explained the rules. 'There will be two heats and the top two from each heat will go into a final. We'll do it just like a real comp. The first group of four gets twenty minutes to catch waves. We'll score every wave, but only your top two will count.'

'Whoever has the most points from those two waves wins the heat. Then, the top two from each heat make the final, which will be scored the same way. Got it?'

It sounded complicated and, in truth, I just wanted to surf. But I also wanted to impress Nick and his friends, so I caught as many waves as I could within the allotted twenty minutes. No matter the size, I went for *everything*.

Back on the beach I strode up to Nick, expecting him to congratulate me on a job well done.

'Don't catch so many waves, you idiot,' he said.

My heart plummeted and heat rose in my cheeks. What the heck was he talking about?

'I thought the whole idea was to catch as many waves as I could.' I took a wide stance, demanding answers.

'Competitions aren't about quantity, bro, they're about quality. You only need two good waves, so don't waste all your effort on crap.'

> **You only need two good waves, so don't waste all your effort on crap.**

The world of competitive surfing opened up to me when I saw a flyer for the Grommet Cup in the local surf shop, at age eleven. It was for surfers under sixteen years old and being held not far from my home beach. Hell, yes! I posted in my entry form and practised like crazy.

Strategy beats talent

Needless to say, I didn't win my first pseudo surfing competition, but I did learn valuable life lessons: talent only goes so far and then you need strategy. By focusing on the important wins, you can avoid spreading yourself too thinly. This means you can be present for and stay focused on the activities you want to spend time on, rather than trying to be everything to everyone. Work smarter not harder to win heats — real and metaphorical.

The day before the competition, I made sure my wetsuit was dry and my board was clean. The competition was obviously a big deal because Dad and Nick were coming to cheer me on, so I wanted to be at my optimal performance. But should I eat eggs for breakfast? What would the pro surfers eat? Should I put my board in the car with the top up or down? What if I do it wrong and a fellow competitor ridicules me? It was a restless night, as I tossed and turned among sweaty sheets.

On the morning of the competition, Dad drove me to the event. It wasn't until the moment I alighted from the car and saw the crowded beach that I realised how big this event was, and cringed.

Other children clearly had parents who surfed, and those parents were waxing shiny new boards for them, deep in conversation about surf conditions and tactics. I tried to swallow a ball of panic that stubbornly stuck in my throat, looking from my second-hand board and non-competition surfer dad to the sleek outfits around me. This wasn't anything like the mock competitions Nick and our mates had organised. I was in way over my head.

Nick had never competed himself, but stepped easily into the coach role, giving me some pointers about picking the right waves, not worrying about what other competitors were doing, and the importance of *not* catching every wave. He also somehow seemed to know what was going on.

'There will be a series of three events with an overall points score,' Nick said. 'All the points add up for an overall series winner.' I stared at my brother, wide-eyed and keen to learn anything that would give me a competitive edge. He kindly didn't remind me that close to a hundred other children were competing, many with a lot more experience.

Then something unexpected happened. Standing in the competitors' area, I took in the hustle and bustle of the competition. A smile spread across my face as Dad and Nick fussed over my preparations. Some other spectators eyed me, like they were sizing up a racing champion. An uncharacteristic warmth bubbled through my veins, and I stood a little straighter, puffed out my chest a little.

Competitors were important people, and *I* was going to compete.

When the time came, I gathered close to the competitor check-in point with three other competitors and donned the brightly coloured lycra vest that had been allocated — a way to recognise me out on the waves.

'Christo Hall,' an official called. I waved my hand and moved closer with my board. I was trying to focus on what I needed to do, just like Nick told me to, but a swarm of butterflies ravaging my belly was making it mighty difficult.

When it was time to stride down the sand towards the water, I made sure the best side of my board was facing the spectators. We were directed to paddle out, so I ran into the shallows, beside the other boys in my heat. Once the water was up to my thighs I sank onto the board, stomach first, and paddled hard. Cool water flowed across my skin. The familiarity calmed me. My mind emptied of noise and worry.

A horn sounded from the beach to signal the start of my heat. We were underway. I felt an urge to get busy and catch lots of waves, but Nick's voice played on a loop in my head. 'Don't catch too many waves! Just get the good ones, don't waste time with bad waves.' So I did my best to remain calm and strike only when the best opportunities came.

Sitting atop my board behind the wave breaks, I watched the ocean and waited for a set of decent waves. This was no different to the hundreds of other waves I'd caught, I told myself. I could totally do this.

When the wave I'd been waiting for arrived, I was ready and didn't hesitate. The wave rose behind me and I thrust my hands into the water at speed. There was a moment when a lip formed on the top of the wave and I started to slide down the face of the wave in a cocoon of silent concentration. And then I jumped up, planted my feet on the board and let the thrill of flying across the water take me. I rode that wave like an eagle flying through the clouds, wrapped in a cloak of certainty as I pushed the board through a series of manoeuvres. As the waved closed in on itself, I climbed the foam and dropped over the back of the swell.

I paddled out to catch more waves.

After twenty minutes, the horn sounded from the PA system, signalling the end of the heat, and I paddled in, oblivious to who'd won. Actually, I didn't especially care as I jogged out of the surf, board under one arm, on top of the world.

'You won! You won!' shouted Nick.

Dad clipped me on the back, beaming with pride. I was already a winner.

To my surprise, I progressed through all of the heats and at the end of the day found myself in the water with the final four competitors. A couple were older and bigger than me — and more experienced.

With longer arms, they managed to paddle past me and get closer to the breaking part of the waves, which meant they had priority for the wave. Even when I started to paddle in, they were faster and more committed. I missed my turn a couple of times. I hung back, becoming increasingly nervous. I didn't want to annoy anyone, but I was also thinking about Nick and Dad on the beach cheering me on.

At the end of the day, I stood third on the podium holding a shiny trophy between my hands, and beaming brighter than the sun.

Surfing was my main obsession from then on, but making money for more boards and more surf competitions was always a close second. Somehow, every dollar I earnt validated my worth in the same way competing did. A significance and a validation came with winning *and* earning money.

> **A significance and a validation came with winning *and* earning money.**

I guess watching my family run small businesses over the years rubbed off on me. It was the only way I knew you could make a living. Mum, importing jewellery from Bali and turning the garage into a storeroom, opening multiple ladies' fashion stores. Dad, in his own accounting firm. And my grandparents, as farmers and plumbers.

Sometimes money was tight and other times plentiful, but I could see the correlation between having it and being able to do more cool stuff and buy more cool things. (People say money doesn't make you happy but that's bullshit. It provides freedom to do the things you love and amplifies the fun things you can do. Then it's up to you to find the balance between making it and enjoying it.) Entrepreneurship was in my DNA; all I wanted to do was surf, but I also had a sense that I would find ways to make my own successful businesses (some day when I was 'grown up').

Lessons from the ocean

It's not about how hard you work; it's about the results you get

In business, people get a bit obsessed with being the hardest-working individual. It's almost become cool to be the busiest, the hardest working. However, all that really matters are the results you get.

To win a heat in surfing all you need to do is catch two waves. To win in business, you need to know which of your products or services are the easiest to sell and which are the most lucrative. Then you need to focus on these like a hawk and build a marketing pipeline to sell them. These offerings need to be highlighted and featured on all of your marketing, and you need to lead people down the pathway of least resistance to convert them from being a viewer to a buying customer. When you have a clear pathway for a customer, the mathematics start to make sense and you can set your advertising budget, increasing it as the sales start to flow.

Towards the end of my full-time competitive surfing, I bought into and ran a surfboard business. From the outset, I knew the fibreglass board industry was too competitive, so we focused on foam surfboards used by mostly beginner surfers. I initially put equal effort into producing every length of board — from the six-foot up to the nine-foot, six-inch option, and in every six-inch increment. I also sold the boards with equal and divided effort to individuals, and to surf shops, resorts and surf schools via wholesale. And I had heaps of ideas to continually expand the product range of surfing accessories we sold.

However, what I realised very quickly was that the learners at the surf schools damaged the boards quicker, which meant they needed to buy boards more regularly. I realised they were ordering more than any other customer base, sometimes forty to fifty boards in a single order. The longer boards had a much higher profit margin than any other board and any accessory, at around $250 per board. Surf schools also want a big stable board, so they can get their students experiencing the thrill of standing up on a board in a single lesson. It was the perfect alignment. Selling the biggest boards to surf schools became 90 per cent of my focus, making buying these boards simple for the customer, so they didn't have to think about too many options.

Once we had this clarity, operations for the whole business were easier and profits became faster to produce. We did initially lose sales by limiting the range, which sounds scary, but it was only a matter of a few weeks before the profits reached new heights.

If you're employed in someone else's business, this translates to finding what makes you most valuable in that organisation and focusing on doing more of that activity. I've had team members working for me who I helped find something specific they were good at, such as managing online ads, managing business automation or creating video content. Through advising them to focus more on being a specialist in those specific areas, they have become experts who can charge more for their work and their skills are transferrable to any business.

Carve your path

The first two questions I ask business owners when I mentor them about ways to get more customers and increases profits are the following:

1. *What are your bestselling products and services, or the most common enquiries you get?* You need to sell people what they want. If you have one hundred products, work out which ones are the highest sellers, because those products will be the easiest ones to get a high return on from your marketing efforts. On the flipside, if you're trying to advertise everything equally, likely some items won't generate any response from prospective customers. You might also need to consider the effect of different seasons. Most people make the mistake of having an advertising budget that they spend equally each month, even though many businesses have better and worse seasons in the year for selling to new customers. If you can recognise better and worse times of the year for selling to your new customers, consider increasing your budget when new customers are looking to buy and lowering your budgets when they're not.

2. *What are your most lucrative products and what makes you the most profit when you sell it?* You need to be clear on this and make sure you get these products in front of customers. You might find that your highest-selling products (identified from the previous question) are also your most profitable. If this is the case, you're in luck—you only need to market that one offering and aim to become known as the 'go-to' business or expert for that thing. On the other hand, you might find that

people who have never bought from you before are very unlikely to buy your most lucrative or profitable item as their first purchase. If that's the case, you might need to sell the most popular offering and then make sure you have a follow-up campaign to promote the most lucrative option, after they've already bought from you and trust you.

Make a list of all of your marketing collateral and find ways to feature your most popular and most profitable offerings. An easy start is to feature these two offerings on the home page of your websites as featured products or services. This means anyone who lands on the home page will see them without having to click through any other pages.

CHAPTER 3
FIRST EUROPEAN TRIP

The most powerful resource to generate success is you!

A trickle of sweat meandered from my hair, down the back of my neck and between my shoulder blades. My thighs burned as I squatted for what felt like the hundredth time, kicked my legs out until I was planking, lowered my chest into a push-up and then jumped to my feet.

'Really brace your core as you snap up,' Nev barked.

I narrowed my eyes at him. Burpees sucked but I refused to surrender.

A rumble of good-natured laughter erupted from Nev's expansive chest. The guy looked more like a middle-aged bouncer than a personal trainer—built like a half-tonne tank with ropes of thick muscle like a powerlifter (which, apparently, he had been once upon a time). I'd heard a story of him throwing someone who'd given him trouble down a staircase; definitely someone you wanted on *your* side.

I started regular training with Nev when I was eighteen and he was a natural motivator, knowing just how far to push me—slightly past where I thought my limits were, but always stopping before I hurt myself or collapsed with exhaustion. Sometimes I could hardly wash my hair after a session because my arms felt like jelly.

'You have to turn your muscles to jelly to turn them to stone,' he said.

That mindset of going for it and leaving nothing on the table sticks with me to this day.

Nev and I developed a good rapport—he wore a necklace with little gold boxing gloves, had a wide jaw, short neck and a flat top hairstyle, but he really was a big softy who wore his heart on his sleeve. And he was one of my biggest supporters, always keen to follow my surfing career and offer priceless motivational quotes like, 'Surf every wave like it's the last wave you'll ever surf'. That mindset of going for it and leaving nothing on the table sticks with me to this day.

In one competition during our time together I was aggressive and interfered with another competitor, meaning I was disqualified from the event. Nev was the only person who was proud of me for that.

Our high-energy trainings meant I was in top physical shape during the next few years of surfing competitions. It's a pity the same couldn't be said for all areas of my personal life. (Hey, I was eighteen years old *and* a pro surfer, living the dream. Of course I took advantage of the limelight and revelry.)

My friends didn't care that I had 5 am starts or a gruelling training regime. They were young and it was time to party hard! I didn't want to miss out and was torn between what I knew I needed to do to succeed, and what I desperately *wanted* to do with my friends. Even the buddies I made on the professional surfing circuit liked to party, so who was I to buck the norm?

It was like balancing on a knife's edge at times: cheating my hard-won gains and letting my dreams slip further away when I drank too much; and then feeling nerves and anxiety weigh me down when I stayed home and focused on nothing but winning.

'All work and no play makes Christo a dull boy,' Mum once said.

But finding the right balance wasn't easy.

Don't get me wrong, I was fully committed to surfing. I hired a surfing coach, Graham, was on the beach every opportunity I got and entered local competitions for extra training.

Working with Graham forced me to confront the need to strategise, not only when I was in the waves, but also before and after each competition. We'd talk through different scenarios, planning for situations when the waves would be consistent and plenty of opportunities would be available in a heat, but also for days when the waves were small or inconsistent and I needed to be patient. It wasn't easy to sit, waiting for a decent ride while others caught wave after wave, but when I found the right one, I sure made it count.

One of the heat simulations Graham would have me run was called 'build a house'. In this I'd practise getting a few quick rides at the start of a heat, to lay a solid foundation for my scores, and then build on that base by waiting for better waves later in the heat.

Understanding the benefits of always having a clear strategy, rather than going into a situation hoping for the best, gave me a stable footing when I started my own businesses. I would build the foundation first and then continually work to improve, knowing that business is like a living thing that you need to continually improve, or it will be going backwards. As long as I could see progress, I could feel mentally motivated.

◆ ◆ ◆

By 1998, at the age of eighteen, I had placed well in a series of Australian junior surfing events and was stoked to have made enough money to enter the European world tour events. It was exciting to be meeting up with friends on the other side of the world, and a little freaky to be going all the way to Europe for the first time.

My main sponsor, Billabong, gave me a few thousand dollars towards travel costs and a bunch of products, so I had all the gear I needed to compete. With flights purchased and $3000 in the bank, fully at my disposal, I assumed I had more than enough to do the tour throughout Europe.

As long as I could see progress, I could feel mentally motivated.

'This is the big leagues, Christo. This feels good. Don't stuff up!' I told myself.

The morning I left for Europe, Mum volunteered to drive me to Sydney Airport. I was flying to France alone. No doubt her motherly intuition had kicked into overdrive when I staggered out of my room with a death-like pallor. My mates had given me one

44

hell of a send-off party the previous night. One of Nick's friends managed the Riva nightclub in the city and gave us the royal treatment, which equated to *way* too many drinks.

'I wish you'd eat some breakfast,' Mum said for the tenth time, then took pity on me and placed a reassuring hand on my shoulder as we got into the car. 'Don't worry. You've trained hard for this.'

'I'm just excited,' I half lied.

The truth was the butterflies that always accompanied a competition were drowning in the litres of alcohol my poor body hadn't yet absorbed from last night. Ugh, just the thought of beer... Why did I do this to myself with a full day of travel ahead of me? At least I could sleep on the plane.

The stop–go motion of the traffic, no breakfast and nerves were playing havoc with my stomach. 'Stop the car, Mum,' I groaned as saliva pooled in my mouth and sweat prickled my forehead.

'Hang on a minute, there isn't anywhere to pull over here.'

'Stop! Stop! Stop!'

The car was boxed in by traffic, but we were slowing for a red light, so I opened the passenger door partway and leaned out before the car had fully stopped. Clear fluid and two undissolved paracetamol tablets gushed onto the bitumen with the force of a fire hydrant.

Mum didn't say a word for the remainder of the drive, but it wasn't like my head had the capacity to worry about what she might be thinking. My skin was hot and clammy and my sight blurred every now and then.

Standing in line to check my luggage at the airport, Mum turned to gaze at me with a disappointed expression. 'You stink of alcohol,

Christo. This isn't how I brought you up. You're not a playboy and you need to straighten yourself up or get a proper job.'

'Sorry, Mum.' What else could I say? She had always been open-minded but I guess even supportive parents have their limits.

Her tone softened slightly then. 'I'm just worried about what's going to become of you if you keep living week to week like this. What are you going to fall back on if the surfing doesn't take off?'

I knew I was going to be successful. I didn't know how yet, but somehow just the belief that I would be successful served me in more ways than I could comprehend at that moment.

'I know. This tour is going to turn things around though, Mum. You'll see.'

'Three months is a long time. Be safe.' She squeezed me in a tight hug and watched me walk through the doors to the passport control area.

The long flight to France gave me plenty of time to reflect on the foolishness of partying right before a competition. Surfing was all I'd wanted to do since I was eight years old and now I had a real chance. Money had been coming in from surfing since I left school and dedicated more time to it — not a lot, but enough to get by while living with my mum. I just needed to be sensible and stay focused. One step at a time, right?

But what Mum had said wormed its way into the deepest recesses of my mind and plagued my subconscious while I slept fitfully on the plane. What if it didn't work out? I had no fallback option. On the other hand, the universe had always had my back in the past and I trusted it to provide opportunities when I needed them. I always made enough money to get by and, at the end of each month, somehow more cash would come my way and keep me going for another month. Still, a professional athlete shouldn't be heading into a world tour hungover.

◆ ◆ ◆

After a 28-hour flight I was exhausted, with eyes so dry they were gritty and burning. Dragging my giant board bag — which looked more like a canoe or body bag — through Bordeaux Airport got a lot of curious stares, and people tended to make a wide birth around me. The shoulder that was looped through the board bag strap was already straining under the weight and, I knew from past experience, would be sore for a few days. Luckily, booking the cheapest possible flight meant I had arrived in Bordeaux two days before any of my surfing buddies. (Anything to make my small amount of sponsorship money go as far as possible.)

I don't know what the customs officers saw, but they took pity on me and waved me through. A face-splitting grin glued itself in place as I headed for the exit. Hell, I was in France and nothing else mattered in this moment. I was here to conquer the world on my own!

There's something magical about travelling overseas. I felt vulnerable, yes, but also exhilarated at the prospect of exploring new places and experiencing new things. All my senses were heightened as I took in the sights, sounds and smells of a new (to me) country.

Pulling out my Lonely Planet guidebook, I studied the route I'd worked out beforehand: walk out of the airport, go to the city loop bus, get off in the town square, and then walk two blocks to the hotel where I would stay for two nights alone. (Once my buddies arrived, we were planning on getting a hire car and heading south to find accommodation near the competition sites in Hossegor.) It sounded easy enough.

I found the bus without incident and used the only French line I'd practised, *'Parlez-vous Anglais?'*

The driver frowned down at me. *'Non.'*

Ah, okay, this was going to be interesting. Now what? Oh well, I needed to get somewhere, so I boarded the bus and let it take me away.

'Excuse me,' the smiling woman next to me said in a French accent. 'I overheard you talking to the bus driver. What stop are you looking for?'

As far as I was concerned, this was another sign that the universe always had my back. With my newfound interpreter handy, I managed to get off at the correct stop. Pity the universe didn't send me a free taxi too.

Two blocks sure seems like a long distance when you're dragging seven surfboards and a travel bag. It's not like I overpacked either. I had a few summer clothes and some essentials — a little set of speakers, a rockstar biography to read and surfing gear for every season.

After a couple of weeks in France and no great results in the first two events, I was frustrated. I'd suffered some bad luck and just missed out on progressing very far. Sometimes the best waves just don't come your way. This is part of the challenge of competitive surfing and part of the magic when it does go your way.

Yeah, well it's not like you're taking this seriously anyway, Bronco nagged. *I mean, make up your mind whether you're a surfing playboy or a pro surfer.*

The next event was in Newquay, in Cornwall, England. The town was buzzing with holidaymakers, and the beach was packed with people enjoying their July summer holidays.

Meeting the inner voice

Bronco is the voice inside my head — the one who reminds me of all my insecurities, and the one who always seems anxious when opportunities arise or fearful of embarrassment.

Bronco was my own internal monster who I needed to overcome before I even got in the water.

When faced with a great opportunity, he'd be there. When required to step outside of my comfort zone, he'd be there. When I was focused on motivating myself to succeed or be resourceful, he was a genius at finding excuses to delay.

On my first trip to Hawaii, he'd been there, but I don't think I was mature enough to recognise the impact he had, so he didn't bother me too much. I could enjoy the freedom of just letting loose and going for my dreams without thinking too much about consequences. Ah, the bliss of being a junior competitor.

Now, I was getting increasingly better results, more sponsorship, and more exposure through photos in magazines and videos. But this meant I had more to lose, and I continuously felt the need to get more.

Once I reached the open age group, my career progression slowed. I could feel the clock ticking on my surfing career and that's when Bronco really made himself known.

I arrived at my accommodation to a very enthusiastic host wearing a checked Ascot tie and matching checked waistcoat over a rotund belly. 'Welcome! I'm 'appy to 'ave you staying with us. You're coming from Australia, is that right?' (Okay, that's my attempt to capture his accent, but hopefully you can picture him now.) He ushered me in, grabbing my small bag and not pausing for a response. 'Come on, come on, let's get you settled then. It's wonderful to have so many international travellers in our village for the surfing event. You look like you mean business there.' He pointed at my board bag.

After getting myself settled, I was keen to check out the surf, so grabbed a board and walked around the town, which was wrapped around a lush golf course, sprawling between two headlands. I guess someone with deeply tanned skin, scruffy blonde hair and a surfboard tucked under one arm stood out in this quaint English village, because people of all ages stopped to say hello and see if I was here for the surfing event, curious about where I was from and when I would be competing, even offering to show me around during my downtime.

Either these were the friendliest people on Earth or the locals were genuinely excited to be hosting the world tour. I could feel the excitement of wanting to party brewing inside me, like a little flame lit up in my belly. *Oh my goodness*, I thought, *this town is gonna be fun.*

Passing a group of women at an alfresco cafe table, and bolstered by the enthusiasm of all the locals I'd already met, I dared to smile directly at them.

An athletic blonde with a clinging dress and a cute smile said, 'Hello there, are you having a good day?'

'Yeah, I've just arrived.' I sidled up to their table.

'Oh, an Aussie,' she said, as though that made me more interesting by far. All the girls giggled and shot meaningful glances at one another. Flicking a stray lock out of her eyes, the blonde asked, 'Do you want to join us for a drink?'

Did I ever! Oh, but I'd made myself a promise after the shit show in France. 'I'd love to, ladies, but I have to behave before the surfing event tomorrow. Later in the week would be awesome, though.'

'Sure.' The blonde smiled coyly. 'Perhaps we'll see you down at the beach?'

I was in two minds about walking away from them but, at the same time, I was proud to stick to my guns and not get caught up drinking this early in a competition week. A positivity I hadn't felt since leaving home flowed through my body. See, I could have the best of both worlds.

It seemed that all I needed to do to enjoy temporary rockstar appeal was to be an Aussie surfer. I didn't need to be the best-looking, tallest or richest bloke; female heads still turned as I walked. Trying not to let this realisation swell my head, I strolled to the esplanade.

A rise at one end of the town provided the perfect view over Fistral Bay. It wasn't a long beach but the rocky headlands protected it and the waves were similar to the messy beach breaks I'd grown up with.

Once down on the beach, I dipped a foot in the water — and then snapped it back out. Geez, I was glad I'd brought my wetsuit. I shook my head at the English families splashing about in the shallows like they were in the tropics.

Not one to let a little frostbite get in the way of a good wave, I bravely ran into the icy water. The shock took my breath away momentarily, but the conditions soon felt familiar, comforting. Soon I was in my element.

◆ ◆ ◆

All eyes were keenly on the competitors all week, whether we were competing, waiting for a heat or enjoying the sights. Groups of children ran up to me now and then to get a T-shirt or signature book autographed, or just to say hello and check out my boards. It was festive.

Early on in the event, I had a couple of good heats and easily progressed through the rounds. Then, just as I was finding my groove on day three, the ocean went flat. After a bit of waiting and hoping, the event organisers announced the competition was on hold indefinitely due to conditions being incontestable. They told us they needed to wait for bigger waves and would be making a call at the start of each day as to whether the competition would run. Not good for my focus.

There was nothing to do but take advantage of the English hospitality. On the first day, I saw some of the local sights. It was an ideal distraction from over-strategising. By the end of the second day, and with the event still on hold, I was ready for some excitement, so I let my new friends lead the way to a nightclub. Needless to say, I staggered back to the hotel in the wee hours of the morning with a lot of booze in my belly.

Naturally, the next morning surf was up and the competition was back on. 'Suck it up, Sunshine. Push through the exhaustion and nausea and get out there to win,' I told myself.

Bronco wasn't as positive. *Nice one idiot. You prepared for months, travelled all the way across the planet to get to this event and then, right when it counts, go out partying.*

A headache thundered around my skull as I entered the water and doubt seeped into my mind.

You're not ready for this. You should be at home building a proper career.

I pushed the negative thoughts aside, but they bobbed up and down in my mind like my board on the water. So, I focused on the cold ocean flowing over my skin, pushing the fog of the hangover away and leaving me invigorated. I'd fought long and hard to get here. I deserved to be here and I would make the most of it. Be present.

The heat started and my energy kicked in. I rushed to catch a few early waves and get a feel for my board in the conditions. Halfway into a twenty-minute heat, I was in second place. All I had to do was hold my position to avoid elimination.

The waves weren't great, so I stayed close to the surfer in third place, trying to block him from any decent waves. My entire focus shifted to preventing him from scoring instead of staying on my own game. It all seemed to work well until the last couple of minutes.

The guy in fourth place caught a fantastic wave and jumped up to second place. Shit, what was I doing, chasing someone else around when I should be looking for my own waves? I desperately searched, looking at every wave and hoping it might give me an opportunity.

'Come on, give me a fucking wave!' I cursed under my breath.

The time counted down and the horn sounded from beach. I was in third place and eliminated from the event.

Dumbfounded, I returned to the beach, charged with anger. 'Shit happens,' I told myself. Sometimes you were just out of sync with the ocean. It's not like the ocean provided an even playing field; I'd seen plenty of talented surfers beaten by poor-quality waves. Every wave had different scoring potential and some simply put you at a disadvantage, no matter how well you surfed.

Feeling hundreds of eyes on me as I walked up the cold sand to the competitors' area, I clenched my fist to prevent it from smashing through my surfboard.

A French surfer nodded at me. 'Unlucky, Christo.'

'Yeah.' I wanted to rip his head off, even though I knew it wasn't *him* I was enraged at.

My mind spun around and around my decision to block another competitor. It was just bad luck, that's all. Then my coach Graham's voice came through as clearly as if he were standing beside me.

'Stay focused on what you need to do.'

No matter how I tried to spin it, I'd left number four alone to find whatever wave he'd wanted. Peeling off my wetsuit, I let the icy tentacles of the breeze raise hairs along my limbs. One discomfort distracting me from another.

You know why you lost, Bronco said. *You couldn't resist partying for a single week.*

Whether I wasn't at my best because of the previous night or because I'd psyched myself out with nerves, didn't matter. It all ended the same and I had no-one but myself to blame. Time and time again, I'd proven I had the skills. I could train hard. I was committed.

Not always, Bronco reminded me. *You really messed up this time.*

With all my gear jammed under my arms, I walked away from the beach, taking deep, relaxing breaths. I was nearly clear of the smiling crowd.

'Hey, Christo, have you got a few words for our viewers?' A television reporter shoved a microphone in my face, eyes and mouth wide with expectation. The lens of a camera glistened on the shoulder of another man. *Sand, engulf me now.* I pulled my grimace into a smile and answered questions about surf conditions and what went wrong.

'Better luck next time, you're a natural on TV,' the reporter said, slapping me on the back. I felt like punching myself in the face for screwing up, but must have hidden it well.

◆ ◆ ◆

Walking through the little coastal town, people smiled and greeted me like an old friend. I did my best to plaster a smile across my face. The moment I'd dumped my gear at the hotel, I paced the room. No way could I stand to be cooped up inside with Bronco all night, so I walked the streets and spotted some friends who were having a beer outside a little bar, soaking up the sun's rays.

A few beers in, I relaxed and started to enjoy the afternoon. So it was, with a sense of self-destruction and the need to silence the internal chatter, one bar led to another and another. It's not like I had to behave myself now that I'd been eliminated, so I might as well cut loose and get the full travel experience.

> **I felt like punching myself in the face for screwing up, but must have hidden it well.**

Leaving the bars, I bought a bottle of vodka to share with a couple of the local surfers who'd taken me under their wing, and headed to one of their apartments. The next thing I remember was kneeling in a dark corner of the garden, heaving. Seemingly distant English accents carried through open windows, asking, 'Where's Christo?'

I can't remember leaving the garden and have no recollection of time passing, but I eventually came back to reality with a sudden slap of noise and sensation. Bodies swayed all around me. A throng of dancers in a club, a bass beat thundering through my feet, smoky air swirling around my head, coloured lights flashing across a crowd of faceless silhouettes. I was in a nightclub.

As sudden as a bolt of lightning, I was sober, aware of myself and everything around me and yet unsure who anyone was. My heart raced as questions about where I was and how much time had passed surfaced. I pushed through the unfamiliar bodies, struggling to find a way out.

Right in front of me, a fight broke out. Two burly men swinging and connecting. Raised voices. A bloody nose. The music still pounding away as people tried to break it up and became entangled in the fight themselves.

A girl stopped next to me to watch. 'So stupid,' she yelled into my ear to compete with the loud music. 'Probably over nothing much.'

We yelled back and forth trying to talk and she picked up on my accent. After a few minutes, she leant over and tried to kiss me, the chaos of the fight still playing out just across the room. I responded with confusion.

The fight drifted closer to us as the girl hugged into me for protection. What the hell had I been up to for the last few hours? And who was this girl hugging up against me? I realised I'd put myself in danger by getting so blotto. I knew I needed to get out of there immediately. Bye.

I found my hotel room and tried to relax, but an angry swarm of wasps buzzed through my mind, stinging me with the reality of what I'd lost on the waves that day.

Lessons from the ocean
The most powerful resource to generate success is you!

Having worked with hundreds of business owners directly, and thousands through my mentoring programs, it has become very clear to me that the mindset of the individual is the biggest driver of success or failure. You can have all the greatest business growth strategies in place, but if you don't have the right mindset you're not likely to succeed. We all need strategies to keep our mind on track.

We all have an inner voice, and this inner voice is a big part of our mindset. How we communicate internally affects how we behave on the outside.

When we see a threat, our inner voice will fire up to keep us safe. The problem is our inner voice will also fire up to keep us safe from feeling uncomfortable — and discomfort is where growth occurs. Usually when we're learning something new or experiencing growth, we're doing something unfamiliar. We feel uncomfortable when we're being pushed outside our comfort zone. And this is often when that inner voice pipes up, outlining all the reasons to get comfortable again.

The inner voice is also a genius at finding excuses not to do things, and often those things are related to health, business growth, sales and education. How easy is it to find a reason not to exercise?!

When I first started public speaking, Bronco (my inner voice) would come up with all sorts of reasons why I would fail, why I'd be happier if I didn't try. But with my experience from competition surfing, I knew he was just a part of me. I also knew the fact that he was there, trying to make me afraid, really just meant a great opportunity was in front of me. When he started chattering away, I knew I was doing the right thing. Even better, I actually started to enjoy the thrill of the fear. I knew I could feel the fear and still deliver an amazing presentation.

Carve your path

◆ Think of something that you've been procrastinating on which you know would be good for your career, health or education. Big ideas might come to mind — such as creating a new business idea, joining a health program, or getting a mentor. But also don't overlook the smaller day-to-day activities you do, and how you might be able to push yourself in these areas. It's often the little decisions you make all day that lead to the big outcomes. Maybe you're avoiding making sales calls by making another coffee every day at 10 am. Or you're not committing to your health by over-analysing options for a gym membership, or waiting till next month to start, or after you've finished a series of TV shows. Perhaps you're not implementing new marketing strategies because you're confused about where to start, so it just doesn't happen. Often this sounds something like, 'Once I get those new business cards/ the new website/social media working, then I'll really get out there and start marketing.' Identify one thing you can take action on now.

◆ Become aware of your inner voice. What does your 'Bronco' say when you think about taking action on the thing you've just identified? To help reassure this inner voice, ask yourself what's the worst that can happen if you do this thing. If the answer is just a bit of embarrassment or potential failure, then proceed. Obviously if real physical harm is possible, you should probably listen to your inner voice.

◆ Be okay with your inner voice trying to stop you from doing things; it's only trying to protect you. And if your inner voice isn't trying to stop you from things, it's likely you're playing too small and staying within your comfort zone. I've found that if you try to tell your inner voice to shut up, it tends to just get louder and smarter at stopping you. So, instead, just acknowledge and thank your inner voice internally. (Don't say this out loud if you're around other people; they'll think you're crazy.) Say something like, 'Thanks for trying to protect me, but I'm going to be doing this anyway.'

♦ I also found that naming my inner voice helped me overcome his nonsense. Maybe you could give yours a name?

CHAPTER 4

AUSTRALIA

Know your purpose

Back in Australia from Europe and England, and in the last year of my teens, I decided it was time to start taking my surfing career more seriously if I was going to make a living from it. So, I started training with my personal trainer, Nev, three times a week, and I ordered some top-quality boards.

Many of the world's top surfers buy boards from Simon Anderson in Brookvale, right around the corner from where I grew up. Simon's craftsmanship is legendary in the industry. He's dedicated to crafting the perfect board to suit each rider. As luck would have it, we surfed the same beach and, after seeing me surf in my early teens, Simon became one of my sponsors.

I was always stoked to receive boards made by Simon (and still am to this day) because each board would be better than the last, improving my performance in the surf. I'd give him feedback on how the last board handled overall and through specific manoeuvres, and Simon would make little adjustments to the shape of the next board. Whether my goal was speed in small waves, the ability to drive harder through turns or big wave riding, Simon would craft a new design with little changes based on my feedback. The average person likely wouldn't notice these subtle differences, but in the water, they changed my approach.

So, before the next round of surfing events, I talked to Simon and ordered custom-shaped boards, allowing plenty of time for me to test and get a feel for them before the competitions.

One of the big events that year was in Margaret River, Western Australia, and it was a good opportunity to gain points and prize money. I arrived at Perth Airport with my Kiwi travel buddy Blair. Billabong sponsored both of us and he'd billeted at my house during a junior competition at North Narrabeen once. We were firm friends from that moment on and chose to travel the world circuit together when we could.

Preparing, and visualising, for success

Surfing events always have a long lead-up time, and preparing for them is an exciting period. Once I turned pro, I tried various preparation formulas to find one that worked for me, such as psyching myself up by listening to high-intensity songs and visualising myself doing well. Like in my childhood fantasies, I would imagine myself riding a monster Hawaiian tube instead of the local small waves. Then, I repeated the process on the event days as a way of curbing anxiety and staying focused on what mattered.

Positive visualisation didn't always work for me, but it took me a while to work out what did (more on that in chapter 7). For now, I needed to work with what I had.

Blair had a heart of gold and a strong sense of what was right and wrong, which proved handy during our travels. Many times we'd find ourselves in situations where it was difficult to tell if someone was trying to rip us off, and I could always count on Blair to speak up if something felt off.

For this event, we rented a van from a low-cost car rental — the company name contained the word 'cheap', which should have tipped us off, but we were on a shoestring budget. The rental yard was full of old, beaten-up cars. At least we wouldn't have to worry about taking the van down dirt roads to get to the best surfing spots. We'd booked a delivery-style van, which was perfect to sleep two in the back if needed and carry our gear; no strapping boards onto the roof.

'It doesn't look like the petrol gauge works,' I said, tapping a finger against the dial.

'What do you expect from a cheap ride?' Blair shrugged. 'We should have enough to get us to Bunbury.'

Brimming with excitement, Blair and I hit the road, the radio cranked up loud, windows open and sunshine coming through the windscreen. A short while later, the van sputtered and lurched.

'Shit, what was that?' Blair hung his head out the window, checking the tyres. 'You think the van's broken?'

We jumped out of the van and looked in both directions along stretches of mostly uninhabited, straight road. Nothing, save for a few abandoned-looking houses.

Blair burst out laughing. 'I love it, the cheap van's dead already.'

I tapped the fuel gauge. 'I just thought the petrol gauge wasn't working, but maybe it really is empty. Oh man, it looks like Cheapy burnt us and only gave us enough to make it to the closest petrol station.'

'Like the one we went past ten minutes ago?' Tears ran down Blair's cheeks as he laughed, leaning against the van and clutching his belly.

I nodded and swallowed down rising panic. This wasn't the kind of smooth start to a journey a responsible, organised adult would have. Of course, Bronco put his two bob's worth in. *You're screwed for sure. This is a sign for the whole event. You're out of rhythm at the beginning and so you might as well quit while you're ahead.*

I clenched my fists and glared at the stationary van. 'Not the smooth start I'd planned. We've barely made it out of Perth.'

Blair suppressed his amusement long enough to take pity on me. 'Hey man, don't stress. We'll get it sorted.' He punched me playfully on the shoulder. 'We're the Cheapy crew. I can just see us walking into Margaret River dragging our board bags behind us.'

Okay, I sniggered a little then. His humour was infectious and the longer he spent doubled over, the stronger the urge to join him was. First, just a chuckle escaped, but soon I lost control and joined him in earnest. It seemed Blair was the fun Yin to my Bronco Yang.

'What now?' I looked from the van to Blair and down the empty road again.

He shrugged, wiping tears from his eyes. 'Push it?'

That just set us both off laughing again, but once our stomachs started to rumble, we put our backs into it and pushed the van along the deserted road. The air was dry, the sky clear and the sun beat down on us. Sweat soon trickled out of my hair and between my shoulder blades. There was nothing but sand and woody bushes either side, with the soil too dry for even grass to grow.

Great, we're never going to make it to the competition and there'll be a news article about the two idiots who ran out of petrol and died in the middle of nowhere.

We managed a good speed, but my limbs were turning to jelly with the exertion. Then finally we saw a petrol station ahead, which gave us a last burst of energy.

Minutes later, we were on our way again. 'Turns out the petrol gauge does work,' I said.

Blair laughed again. 'Margaret River here we come.'

◆ ◆ ◆

Margaret River's main break is renowned as one of the most consistent big wave surfing destinations in the world—and it certainly didn't disappoint for our visit.

Standing on the beach on my first competition day, the breeze blowing briny spray into my face, the three-storey waves were imposing to say the least. In fact, they were enough to strangle the breath in my lungs and make me doubt my sanity. It had been a while since I'd surfed such huge waves.

Shit, I hadn't brought a long enough board for these monsters. Luckily, a friend had a board he could lend me.

> **The three-storey waves were ... enough to strangle the breath in my lungs and make me doubt my sanity.**

Normally, I'd go for a quick surf to get a feel for the conditions before competing, but it just wasn't possible this time. The waves were breaking a long way out and competitors were difficult to spot between the walls of water. I needed to conserve every ounce of energy if I was going to have a chance of making the long paddle out and enduring the impending beatings from the giant waves.

The carpark at Surfers Point near the mouth of Margaret River was the staging area for the competition, and crowds of spectators gathered nearby. This headland provided an excellent view over the ocean and, as I was getting ready, I sat up there and contemplated various strategies for my heat.

I could try to catch a quick wave at the start, and then take my time to get back out, but I'd be lucky to get a second wave in the time it would take me to paddle back out. Everyone would be facing the same challenge, though, and points only counted from each person's best two rides, so I only needed two good waves. Patience, I counselled myself. There was no point in rushing onto smaller waves or putting myself in the way of a monster and being smashed like shell grit without even getting a wave.

The main break played out like a movie in front of my vantage point, and I had a clear view of the massive waves rolling over an underwater rock platform, surging towards shore and finally dissipating in the relative calm of the deep channel to the right. From there, the powerful current of the rip moved the water back out to sea. The channel would be a good tool for getting out fast — so long as I had the energy to pry myself from the grasp of the rip — but if I wanted any hope of making it back to shore, I needed to stay out of the channel and put myself in the firing line of the monster waves.

A couple of jet skis bobbed out of reach of the breaking waves. They weren't there to tow competitors onto the waves, though, like in the giant waves around the world such as Maui in Hawaii; they were purely there to assist in rescues. Today, we'd need to gather all of our strength and training to catch these waves.

You're gonna get your ass kicked by the ocean today, Bronco warned.

'Fuck off,' I told him inside my head. I could do this. Stay positive and catch two good waves, that was my plan. Don't take crap, don't worry about other competitors, just catch two waves and make them count. And get back to shore alive. Simple.

When the loudspeaker announcement called for my heat to check in, I sculled an energy drink and let adrenaline surge through my veins. Nervous energy made the world shrink around me as though all eyes were watching me, waiting for me to succeed or fail. My heart thundered in my chest.

'Good luck,' I called to three fellow competitors at the water's edge.

We paddled out together, but my mind quickly focused on the water in front of me, pushing out thoughts of rescued surfers from a previous heat, strategies other competitors may have and the spectators and news crews on land. It was me against the ocean now.

Nervous energy made the world shrink around me as though all eyes were watching me, waiting for me to succeed or fail.

The borrowed board was unfamiliar beneath me, but I settled into a rhythm. Once the other competitors had found a position to wait for a wave, I kept paddling, way out to where the biggest waves were breaking. After all, I'd rather ride a big wave than have it break on me. So, I paddled further than anyone else, past mountains of water.

Once I was far enough past the breaking waves to be safe, I straddled the board and turned to look back towards shore. Land was a long way off and I couldn't spot the other competitors among the huge waves. It sure was lonely this far out, surrounded by deep black ocean and help a long way off.

It took a few minutes to settle my breathing after the exertion. Just in time to see the red flag on the beach drop and a green flag go up, signalling the start of the thirty-five-minute heat. It was go time.

Limbs tense and at the ready, I bobbed on the water, scouting the horizon for the right swell. Wave after average wave came and went. Now what?

I rubbed my thighs to keep them warm and drummed my fingers restlessly on the fiberglass under me, hearing the minutes tick by in my mind. Maybe I'd be better off paddling in and catching a smaller wave to make sure I was one of the two competitors who progressed to the next round. 'No,' I told myself, 'stay calm and be smart. Stick to your strategy. The other competitors will be struggling to get a wave too.'

After about eight minutes — which felt like an eternity — the horizon disappeared behind some big swells. The first wave reared up out of the black sea but there was a darker swell behind it. Now was my time.

I lay down on the board and paddled even further out, meeting the waves head-on. Sensing their power build, I knew was in a good position. I went over a huge swell and immediately spotted the monster lurking behind. This was it … do or die.

I swung the board around to face the shore and plunged my arms down into the icy water, pulling as hard as I could to get momentum, desperate to meet the wave's speed. It was impossible to guess where these big waves would break, so I was going by feel, aiming for a hundred-metre area and hoping for the best. There was a moment of uncertainty as I rose above the horizon … and then the board gained speed on the water's surface and I was hurtling towards the beach. I was on.

I felt a rush of speed as I jumped up and rocketed down the face of the seemingly endless wave. This adrenaline high only lasted seconds on regular-sized waves, but today it was more like pushing a snowboard down the side of a mountain. I felt like I was riding an endless wall of water. Time was suspended. The moment stretched for so long that a string of jumbled thoughts meandered through my mind like a strange dream.

Still getting a feel for the board, I moved my weight onto my toes to turn along the wave face, and the long board responded beautifully. I glided near to the top of the wave and then carved back down again. The sheer speed and height of the wave meant my main aim was just to survive it — competition points would have to come second — but I did manage a couple of drawn-out turns that covered a few hundred meters.

I rode the wave all the way across the bay until I was in the deeper channel, well away from breaking waves. This left me a long way out to sea but at least I was out of harm's way. It was difficult to see the event site and the commentary coming over the loudspeakers was a distant mumble between breaking waves. The tone seemed more frantic than the usual reading of scores and time remaining, but nothing was going to derail my concentration today.

I checked my watch. Time for another wave. So, I paddled into the abyss again, pumped with adrenaline.

Near the end of the heat, I managed to catch one last ride. It was another monster and sapped my remaining energy. I had no intention of getting stuck in the rip now that my limbs felt boneless from exertion, so I angled the board back towards the break and rode it all the way to shore and safety.

As soon as I neared the beach, I could tell something was up. All of the eyes in the crowd were trained on some action out to sea, at the back of the channel. I was happy to be on land.

'Awesome ride, mate,' said one spectator, clapping me on the shoulder as I passed.

'What's going on?' I lifted a hand to shade my eyes and followed the collective gaze. The two jet skis were rushing towards the right of the main break.

'Two guys from the heat before yours are still stuck out there,' the guy next to me said. 'The poor bastards were sucked out by that rip and have been battling the current trying to get back to shore this whole time.'

Wow. My heat lasted thirty-five minutes and they had been going backwards, being sucked out to sea by the powerful rip, that whole time. All that power from the massive surf had to escape somewhere, so it gouged the channel and flowed out to sea like a strong river. The distance made the men look as tiny as ants, only sighted every now and then as they bobbed over swells. Barely able to place one foot in front of the other myself, I understood their exhaustion and the panic they must be feeling. A collective sigh went up when the jet skis reached the men and cheers once they arrived back on land.

Three-time world surfing champion Andy Irons was telling the media he'd had one of the worst beatings of his life out there that day, which was a big call coming from a Hawaiian who revelled in giant surf. Shortly afterwards, the loudspeakers crackled to life again and the commentator announced the event was on hold for the rest of the day due to the dangerous conditions. It was a relief to finally sit down in the staging area and rest my weary body.

Blair came over and high-fived me. 'Holy shit, I thought you were gonna die for sure out there.'

'What was my score?' I hadn't even had the energy to check.

'You haven't seen? You scored eight for the first wave!'

Eight out of ten, without much in the way of fancy manoeuvres. Usually only a nice wave with a series of impressive manoeuvres would score seven or more. This score really was for me just hanging on and making it across the thing. I guess that shows how big the wave looked from the beach.

This was a good day. I was happy to progress through the event that day knowing the conditions were forecast to be smaller and more manageable for the remainder of that week.

The value of a higher purpose

After a rocky start getting there, Margaret River taught me an important lesson. Having a higher purpose—in this case, wanting to gain rankings points to progress my career—could push me beyond my usual limits.

This would be a lesson that would serve me well in future business endeavours, not to mention being the first viable way I'd found to battle Bronco. Sure, I had to live with him inside my head, trying to undermine everything I did, but I realised I didn't have to accept this part of me that I hated the most. Bronco expresses my ego and insecurities, but I'd silenced him that day at Margaret River. At least for one afternoon, I had silenced the mind chatter. The voice inside my head was quiet.

Lessons from the ocean
Know your purpose

The first thing I do with any business owner I mentor is assist them with getting very clear on their purpose—and I don't mean making money or anything to do with their personal goals. By knowing their purpose, I mean working out exactly what it is the business is really setting out to achieve. How will the business make the world a better place, or life better for its customers? People buy into the outcomes they want—they don't really care about *what* or *how* you do something, but they care a lot about the outcome that gives them. No-one wants another business that sells the same stuff as everyone else—they don't need another accountant, bikini brand, consultant or sunglasses brand. So you need a big purpose that clearly explains why your business needs to exist.

Of course the products and services you offer will affect what your purpose is, but the important part to remember is that customers are less interested in the *thing* you do and more interested in *why* you do it. People are drawn to big ideas, and a big attractive purpose. For example, if you sell mattresses maybe your purpose could be something like, *Every day we strive to change the world by giving you a better night's sleep, more energy and a healthy body. All our products are so exciting we guarantee they'll quickly send you to sleep!*

Once my clients are clear on their purpose, we will use it in their marketing to grab the attention of customers. We'll also display it within the business, so team members know the purpose they're setting out to achieve. Team members should know if they're doing something that moves the business closer to the purpose. Their job then becomes much easier. If a task moves the business closer to the purpose, do it; if something doesn't move things closer to the purpose, don't do it.

Having this big-picture purpose will not only attract customers, but also help you and your team understand the importance of what you do and stay motivated, even when things get tough, which they certainly will at some point in business.

Start with something like, *We're transforming the confidence of women by*…, *We're changing the lives of business owners by*…, *We make the world a healthier happier place by*… You get the idea! If your purpose is big enough and grand enough, you can even change products and services and the big-picture purpose will still be relevant, so think big.

As an example of this, I worked with an Australian-based travel and events company through the pandemic in 2020 to 2024. Their purpose was focused on creating *memorable experiences*. Of course, throughout the pandemic, with lockdowns and other restrictions, they couldn't sell travel and their usual events had to stop, but they could adjust their events—they could do smaller and online events that still fulfilled the purpose of creating memorable experiences. The purpose stayed the same, even though the services changed.

If you're employed or you have a personal brand, you can focus on your personal purpose. Think about this personal purpose. What are you here on Earth to achieve?

Having a sporting career can make articulating a purpose easy, because you do have one thing you were born to do. You have a natural talent. A gift from the universe. Something you love to do every day, which makes total sense to you. The pathway is simple: win and keep improving. All I had to do was be as prepared as possible for the next event, taking them one at a time.

However, many professional athletes have a massive crash when their sporting career comes to an end. Partly this is because they skipped the whole picking a career thing and went straight from school to sports. But mostly it is because they also lose their purpose in life.

Being passionate and knowing your purpose puts you miles ahead of the majority, because it provides you with a focus most people lack, no matter their technical skills. Possessing a qualification proves the ability to complete a job, but is nothing compared to being excited about what you're doing.

Many of the best team members I've hired in my businesses weren't formally trained for their role. If someone is trained in marketing, but their real passion is for running events, then I want them in an events role. Or, if they have no formal education but are more passionate than a candidate with tonnes of qualifications, I'll always hire based on the passion.

Skills can be taught, but passion comes from within—and that passion comes from knowing your purpose.

Carve your path

- If you own a business, consider the *outcomes* people get from your products or services. Make a list of the beneficial outcomes customers get, and then prioritise those benefits in order of what your customers want the most. You want to be clear on at least the top two.

- As an individual, think about your highest impact work — what do you do that really delivers the most value?

- For your business, create a purpose statement that includes the top two to three benefits you deliver to your customers. You can see in the example I provided above three specific benefits to the customer were highlighted: *a better night's sleep, more energy, and a healthy body.*

- As an individual, get clear on your personal purpose. What is your personal purpose here on Earth? What are you here to achieve? What is your specialty? What are your unique skills? What do you want to achieve? Articulate this in one or two sentences.

CHAPTER 5
INDONESIA
Look where you want to go

I landed in Indonesia during the sweltering dry season of 2000 for a month of promotions and competitions. First stop was a remote corner of Sumatra for a week-long photo shoot with a small crew to create an adventure surf trip story for *Waves* surfing magazine, and additional photos to be used for advertisements.

The shoot turned out to be a glorious week spent surfing amazing waves, surrounded by lush greenery dripping from the tangled branches and buttress roots of the jungle, and the perfect opportunity to acclimatise to the local conditions before competing. Indonesia boasts some of the best surf on the planet, with long coral reefs shaping perfect waves and warm water that made it comfortable to stay wet all day.

The *Waves* crew took some spectacular images from land, boat and swimming in the water with us, and later produced a great feature article. The shoot put me in a positive frame of mind for the coming competition. The holiday atmosphere and anticipation of meeting up with familiar faces also had me excited.

At the time, air travel within Indonesia was notoriously unpredictable and the island of Nias, where the event was being staged, didn't have regular flights to it. So, I flew to Medan in North Sumatra, where event organisers were chartering two planes to transport competitors. Thankfully, when I got there I was on the first flight and didn't have to wait another day.

No matter how often I flew, I always felt a little knot of anxiety in the pit of my stomach on unfamiliar airlines. Maybe it was all the rushing around in unreliable taxis panicking because you couldn't afford to miss a flight, or dealing with unexpected changes to schedules, or being forced to put your life in the hands of a faceless airline in a foreign country. Or maybe it was a combination of everything.

Shading my eyes as I walked through the haze shimmering above the scorching tarmac, I spotted the small, rickety-looking plane I was about to board. My only hope was that we'd stay in the air long enough to reach the island of Nias.

I smiled at the letters on the tail: SMAC.

'Great, we're flying SMAC airlines,' I said to Blair, who was travelling with me.

He looked up 'What the hell? The paint's peeling off and everything.' He grimaced.

We climbed the stairs and stepped into the cabin, feeling like we were stepping back in time into an aviation museum piece. The arm rests still had ashtrays, the many cigarettes smoked over the plane's life no doubt the reason for everything in the cabin having faded to a creamy yellow. Tiny fans were suspended from the ceiling above each seat — the limit of technology.

The knot in my belly tightened as a self-preservation alarm sounded in my mind. Naturally, it triggered Bronco. *This is fully sketchy. This thing might fall out of the sky.* I ignored him. I had to get to Nias to compete and this was the only way. At least if the plane went down, I wouldn't be alone.

As everyone took their seats, I distracted myself by chatting to the guy across the aisle. 'What's the padlock for?' I gestured to a robust padlock clipped to the side of his backpack.

> **The knot in my belly tightened as a self-preservation alarm sounded in my mind.**

He grinned. 'I know how things can work in Nias, bro. This is for my cabin door, and I hold on to the only key.'

Shit, I'd never heard about this before and hadn't brought a padlock.

'That's a bit of overkill, don't you reckon?' I said to Blair.

'I can't see anyone stealing from us, it would be too obvious in a small village, but I have heard of people being attacked with machetes here. It's pretty wild.'

The flight crew dragged heavy board bags down the aisle to the back of the cabin — apparently there wasn't enough room in the hold. This was followed by a whole lot of laughing and movement in the back, so I turned to check out the situation.

'Well?' Blair queried. I shrugged and stood to get a better view.

'You won't believe it,' I said. 'Passenger seats have been folded up to make room for the boards and one poor guy is without a seat. He's perched on a pile of life vests tied together with a strap.'

Blair and I exchanged a significant glance, thankful for small mercies like a proper seat with a seat belt. It was highly likely those were the only life vests on board, but at least we knew where to find them ...

As the plane was readied for take-off, the acrid scent of jet fuel filtered through the air vents, roiling my stomach further. Each muscle in my body tensed as the white noise of the engines reached a crescendo. Being a small plane, the engine noise was loud, and even the power of the forward projection could be felt shuddering through the fuselage.

We made it into the air and were soon (although it didn't feel soon enough) preparing for landing. The airstrip in Nias was short and flanked by jungle and mountains, so, on the approach, the pilot took the plane low enough to graze the tops of some palms, their fronds flapping around like crazy from the backwash ripping at them. My eyes bugged wide as I stared out the window at the ground racing below and the impregnable face of rugged mountains at the other end.

At the last second, the pilot abruptly pulled up, aborting the landing and coming around for a second attempt. By this time, all passengers had a white-knuckled grip on the arm rests. Some were mumbling hurried profanities.

On the second attempt, the wheels touched down and it felt like the pilot immediately slammed on the brakes. Bodies were flung forwards with force. We avoided overshooting the end of the runway by a fraction and I breathed a sigh of relief once I was on the tarmac again.

'Longest hour and a half hour of my life,' Blair commented as we disembarked. 'I'm not looking forward to the flight back.'

Binaka Airport on Nias was more like a strip of bitumen in an unkempt paddock, surrounded by waving coconut and banana palms. Next to an abandoned concrete building, we collected our luggage from a pile on the tarmac before piling into minibuses with not much more than duct tape holding the seats together. A theme was emerging here and I wasn't sure I liked it.

◆ ◆ ◆

The next morning, I awoke in paradise with the sound of the waves washing over the reef right in front of our bamboo hut. I brushed my teeth, standing on the decking and looking down at Sorake Beach. The beady telescopic eyes of a sand crab watched me from the beach below, antennae testing the air.

Blair caught me talking to the crab a short while later. 'You right there, bro?'

'Just making friends with the locals.' I grinned and waved at the next in a procession of locals and surfers who walked along the beach in front of our hut.

We didn't waste time before hitting the beautiful mid-sized waves, sans wetsuits thanks to the tepid water. By the time Blair and I were dry, the second planeload of competitors had arrived.

''Sup boys?' a familiar, bronzed Californian asked as we walked back to our hut. I'd recognise the easy smile of Jay Moriarty anywhere. He'd dedicated his life to big wave surfing and was well on his way to legend status at the age of twenty-one.

'Livin' the dream, bro.' I flashed him a thumbs up.

'Did you hear about the plane today?'

Blair and I shook our heads.

'Halfway from Medan it lost an engine, dude.' Jay's usually easy-going nature became animated. 'Half an hour before landing I was lookin' out the window and the propeller fuckin' stopped!'

'Whaaat?' He had my full attention.

'Ninety of the world's best surfers could've gone down in one accident, dude. Can you imagine? The pilot had to turn around and make it all the way back to Medan with *one propeller* because there's nowhere to repair it on Nias. I tell you, dude, it was bloody silent on that plane.'

I instantly had a full body sweat, as sympathetic terror kicked in. 'Everyone okay?'

'Yeah, except for the skid marks. The organisers had to get a military plane to bring us over.'

This did not bode well for our return journey.

◆ ◆ ◆

A few days later, after a full day of surfing events, I was sitting on the deck of our cabin playing cards with a few other Australian surfers. We'd settled into the lazy pace of island life, stepping straight onto the beach and into the surf, and enjoying the convenience of the landlord's family living directly behind the cabins and taking care of our every need.

The dodgy flights over were the talk of the town, especially after an update from the mainland. While the broken propeller was being repaired, the good engine also died. So, the plane was completely out of action. I can't say I was sad knowing I wouldn't have to catch it on the return flight.

In the middle of a hand of cards, our host yelled, 'Christo, is this one okay?'

He was holding a live chicken upside down by the legs, and it was kicking and flapping to free itself. I stared blankly for a minute, and he waited expectantly. Then it dawned on me. Blair had put in a special request for a chicken dinner. That chicken was going to be our dinner.

A shocked laugh spluttered from my lips, and my bewildered friends joined in. I felt sorry for the chicken and sorry for our host, who had no idea why we were laughing. He'd probably gone to great efforts to catch his prize chicken.

Eventually, I managed, 'Yes, that's excellent. Good chicken. Thank you.' Then I whispered to Blair, 'This is all your fault.'

Blair was fussier with his food than me and often survived on toast with peanut butter while travelling — he wasn't keen on many vegetables or salad. Tonight's dinner would scar him for life. It turned out to be the worst chicken dinner we'd ever had. It was stringy with very little flesh and would have been better off left to roam free; poor chicken.

◆ ◆ ◆

The next day, a crazed-looking man showed up outside our cabin, covered in grazes and bloody bandages. His eyes were bloodshot and darting from side to side as though expecting an attack at any moment. I suspected he was high on pain killers and watched him warily from a chair on the deck of our cabin.

After a lot of shouting and wild gesticulation, he made his way onto the balcony waving a syringe around. Blair and I leapt to our feet, ready to fight or flee, as needed. Thankfully, the landlord arrived, explaining that his brother had been in a motorbike accident. Unfortunately, however, it wasn't the last we saw of him. He showed up at random times during our stay, leaving us on edge each time.

On our final morning on the island, everyone was tense in expectation of the flight home. At least we'd heard the organisers were using local military planes this time. To relax our nerves, Blair and I locked up the cabin and headed out for a final surf. We returned refreshed, but the moment I stepped inside the door,

I stilled. The mosquito net over my bed was hanging loose. In the tropics, rule number one was to tuck your mosquito net under the mattress to keep flying things out. Some of my clothes were strewn on the floor, when they'd been neatly packed before we left.

'Shit, someone's been in here,' I said, announcing the obvious.

Blair walked around the ransacked belongings, checking for anything that was missing. I followed suit.

'My cash and watch are gone,' I said.

'I'm lucky. They didn't find my cash stash in the bottom of my toiletries bag.' Blair came out of the bathroom, holding the little black sack aloft.

I jumped at a knock on the door. The landlord had come to collect the final accommodation payment and I told him what had happened. He denied knowing anything about it and the conversation deteriorated into an argument — me red-faced and incensed, and the landlord gesticulating and speaking rapidly switching between English and Indonesian.

A suspected thieving landlord was one thing (I had no proof, but couldn't see who else it could have been in the small community), but when his crazy brother showed up, things took a turn for the worse. He was sweating profusely, and the patchwork of blood-soaked bandages was now grubby around the edges, grazes yellowing and moist. He stepped right up close, leaning into my face, glaring at me with eyes so bloodshot and erratic he could've passed for a zombie.

Spittle sprayed from his mouth as he yelled gibberish. The only word I understood was 'problem', but his body language was plenty clear.

Bronco piped in with a warning. *This guy is batshit crazy and you* do not *want to be on the wrong end of a machete. Don't push him.*

He was right. I had no chance of getting my money or watch back. Better to get out of there in one piece.

I also remembered some advice my surf coach had given me: 'Don't get caught up in arguments with other competitors unless it's part of your strategy. You have a bigger purpose, so don't get caught up in others' nonsense. Rise above it. Always focus on where you want to go.'

> **I had no chance of getting my money or watch back. Better to get out of there in one piece.**

I knew I needed to rise above the situation in front of me. My cash would come and go and I'd been given the watch by a sponsor.

Learning to rise above

When I teach people to surf, I always tell them to look where they want to go (while always keeping one eye on the ocean, of course). Learner surfers will often make the mistake of looking where they *don't* want to go and, therefore, they go there. A learner surfer might be on a wave, travelling at speed, and they want to avoid colliding with someone who is closer to shore. They usually look at the person and this shifts their direction, so they're soon pointing straight at the person they really didn't want to hit.

The same happens in business—people look at all things that could go wrong, and take their eye off where they want to be. It's good to be aware of potential risks, but the most successful businesspeople I've worked with are very solution-focused. Always focus on finding a solution that moves you close to your goals.

(continued)

What you focus on you tend to get more of—and I've found this to be true in surfing and in life. So you definitely don't want to focus on worst-case scenarios.

In a strange way, surfing is like an amplification of your internal thoughts and energy; any turn of the head or shift in focus will change your experience on the wave. Look where you want to go!

The landlord took his brother by the arm and walked him backwards towards his house out the back. I was still pissed off and hated feeling powerless, but I knew, as isolated as we were, the usual laws didn't apply.

'You went through my stuff and stole from me. You can keep it, but I know you're a thief,' I said in a calm tone. The humidity felt even heavier with foreboding as we stared at one another for a silent moment.

Blair tossed enough money to cover both our accommodation onto an outdoor table, and then made a beeline for our bags. We made a speedy getaway to where other surfers had gathered to meet the buses.

◆ ◆ ◆

The competitors were unusually subdued during the bus ride, no doubt dreading the flight back to the mainland. With no air-conditioning on the bus, sweat dripped down the back of my neck and my shirt stuck to my back.

Arriving at the sad little airport building did nothing to lift my mood, and nor did sweltering in the heat for two hours. I wanted *out* of the place. The sound of propellers got everyone on their feet and looking to the sky, eager (I wasn't sure that was the right sentiment) to see what sort of plane was going to show up. Despite the cloud cover, the day was glary and a line of nervous surfers sheltered their eyes as a grey shape solidified in the distance.

'Let's hope they didn't manage to fix that old bucket of bolts that brought us here,' someone said, prompting a few sniggers.

Two planes came into focus. They were short, plump-looking military planes that looked more like cargo carriers than passenger planes. At least they looked well-maintained and solid.

This wasn't like a commercial flight where someone checks you in and a crew settles you in. It was a free-for-all. People just sat wherever they wanted in the two columns of seating. Again, the massive board bags were a problem. Once the cargo hold was full, several rows of seats were given over to them and the giant bags were stacked up to the roof. Unfortunately, that meant there weren't enough seats for people again.

With no crew to find a solution, people were left standing in the aisle. I offered the arm rest of my aisle seat to a friend, but as the plane took off people struggled to stay on their feet, grabbing headrests either side as they braced against the g-forces of lift-

Fear can preserve life, but it can also lead to avoiding opportunity.

off. We made it back to mainland Sumatra without incident, but I've never seen so many surfers relieved to be on dry land.

In business I see risk every day. The time spent on any task, employing someone new, buying stock — these are all risks. Any action or item is a risk. They're all expenses, and all can drain you.

Certain risks in life are real danger, but most risks in business are perceived the same way by us — they trigger fear. Fear can preserve life, but it can also lead to avoiding opportunity.

Lessons from the ocean
Look where you want to go

I had a customer who appeared to be trying to short-change us over $16 000 for mentoring work we had provided for her. The team member who was managing the customer came to me, freaking out. She was really stressed, most likely thinking I would totally lose my cool at her for not managing the customer properly and not following the usual process of getting the payment upfront. She explained the customer had promised payment, but then missed the payment date. They had also not responded to any calls or emails over the last week, when previously they had been very responsive. I looked my team member in the eyes and took a big deep breath, a way for me to relax, become present to her and give myself a moment to think before I responded.

I asked her what the most recent communication had been and what outcome we wanted. I then suggested that maybe the customer needed more time to get the cash or to top up her credits cards with enough to pay the outstanding amount. I explained that business was like a roller-coaster and it might just be a case that they were waiting on a customer to pay them, so they could pay us. The customer might also be embarrassed because they didn't have the cash that minute, and that was why they weren't responding. A lot of variables come up in business. I wasn't trying to make excuses for the customer, but I did want my team member to be open to different thinking. The last thing I wanted was for her to become aggressive towards the customer and make the situation worse. We've had so many situations over the years where people have been late with a payment, which they paid when they could, and then went on to be awesome customers for years to come. I wanted my team member to be calm and get clear on where we wanted to go.

She looked me in the eyes with a questioning look and said, 'You just go through life like Buddha. Why doesn't anything bother you?' I said, 'Whether we get the money or not, we don't need to stress. I won't waste time worrying, one way or another. Just promise me you'll do what you can?' All we could do was find the next step to stay focused on what we wanted, and not get distracted from other progress we were making in other areas of business.

She calmly followed up and messaged the customer, carefully explaining the situation this had put her in within her job. The customer messaged back straightaway to apologise for her silence and explained that her credit card had been blocked for fraud. She was waiting for the new card and asked for more time. Problem solved.

Carve your path

◆ What triggers you with unnecessary reactions? Try to think of a time when you reacted unhelpfully. Or think of the kinds of situations when you regularly react in a way you wish you didn't. If running a business, this could be when a customer questions the quality of your products. In your personal life, this could be when the kids get home from school and you yell at them. Or maybe when you arrive at your business, you already start to feel anxious before you open the door. What is it that triggers you?

◆ Take a moment to think about how you want to feel in these situations that trigger you. How would you prefer to behave in these situations? How do you want to show up for yourself, your family, your partner and your team? Be clear on how you want to be.

◆ Next, practise changing your state. When you feel like you are going to react negatively, or complain, or you know you're coming to a situation where you usually react, take a moment to review. Take three deep breaths. (If someone is standing in front of you, they will wait.) Know that you can change your state at any moment. Maybe go outside and make loud chicken noises to break the pattern. Maybe think of your favourite song for a moment to change your mood. Maybe put your favourite song on before you walk into the office or home. Find what works for you and practise it. You might not nail it the first time, but keep practising.

◆ Most importantly, become aware of your emotional state and the fact that you can change it.

CHAPTER 6
MALDIVES
Routines are magic

Right in front of my home about 700 metres out to sea is a submerged reef shelf, which creates big waves in the middle of the ocean. A First Nations name for these kinds of deep-water breaks is 'Bombora'. The locals call the one near me 'Northy Bombie', and it has a mythical-monster kind of folklore around it.

Even with hundreds of world-class surfers in the area, you only ever find half a dozen crazy enough to attempt the Bombie. Maybe what puts people off is paddling out across nearly a kilometre of deep, dark abyss, imagining white pointer sharks lurking beneath. Or perhaps it's the exhaustion of going all that way and then still having to push through enormous waves on the inside sandbank before you even get to make the long paddle to the catchable waves further out — and experience the sheer rush of gliding down a wave the height of a two-storey building.

But the power of the uniquely shaped waves produced as water passes over the reef and steepens is too much for some. Many surfers have attempted it, only to have the giant waves in front of the Bombie repeatedly wash them back to shore until they're exhausted and give up. Others have gotten stuck out there and had to be rescued by a jet ski.

The thrill of surfing the Bombie has always got the better of me, and one day when the waves were huge I paddled out. After ploughing through the broken white water of the beach-break waves, I was faced with unpredictable fifteen-foot waves pounding the sandbank in front of me, creating a formidable barrier to prevent me getting out beyond the break. Doing so would test my athletic ability and focus to remain calm, but I had seen a few other surfers floating behind the Bombie, so I knew it was doable. I shook out my already tired arms and braced for battle.

I had been so excited about the big waves that I had rushed out and hadn't prepared properly.

I was prepared for the first few waves, standing on my eight-foot big-wave board so I could dive deep under each one to avoid the turbulence and conserve energy. But the waves were unrelenting and my limbs fatigued.

As the next monster loomed over me, I didn't have enough energy to jump onto the board, so held the back of it like a floatation device. The force of the wave ripped the board from my hands, picked me up and tossed me through the air and into the water. Held under, white water tumbled me like a ragdoll in a washing machine. End over end. Losing track of which way was up.

Why the fuck didn't you wear your floatation vest, hissed Bronco.

I usually did wear a purpose-build vest with thin foam inserts when surfing waves that big. These kinds of vests provide a little bit of extra flotation help to bring you back to the surface. Unfortunately, I had been so excited about the big waves that I had rushed out and hadn't prepared properly. I knew I should have warmed my body up more and been wearing my vest.

Bursting through the surface for a moment, I gulped a lungful of welcome air before the next big wave crushed me.

Wave after wave pressed me into the blackness, allowing me only brief breaths before forcing me down again and sucking me back into the danger zone. My fingers were tingly as all energy drained from them, and the strange sensation then flowed along my arms and down my body, all the way to my feet.

Bronco yelled, *Swim you bastard. You're oxygen-deprived and your body is shutting down. Get air. Get air. Get air!*

But I no longer had control of my body — and the worst part? It didn't feel so bad, kind of like I imagine being high as a kite would feel. The next wave was as unyielding as a two-storey building crashing over me, beating me into a limp pile of skin and bones that spun uncontrolled in the vortex of white water.

My brain at least had enough energy left to send increasingly urgent signals for my lungs to breathe. My diaphragm spasmed and I opened my mouth to suck a little air. Salty water rushed in, so I resisted the urge to suck more. This normal physical need was what free divers fought through in order to remain under water longer.

A misplaced calm descended over me. Black spots danced before my eyes. And thoughts of my girlfriend and family passed through my mind. They were going to be pissed at me taking this risk.

I'm sorry. Sorry the pull of the ocean is so strong in my veins that I can't help but give into it, like an addict. A selfish act to please myself. In search of an adrenaline high, even when it's dangerous. I'm sorry.

On average, most people can only hold their breath for around a minute; with training, specialists can manage three to seven minutes. But when you're coping a beating, the oxygen in your system depletes rapidly.

My heart should have been thundering in my chest, and yet it had slowed. If this was drowning, it wasn't so bad — succumbing to the ocean I loved. While the thought of wanting air and not being able to get it is terrifying, in that moment I wasn't scared at all.

I couldn't fight anymore, so let my limbs go limp, sinking into blackness with silver sparkles dancing all around me. The water became calmer as I pushed out to sea. With no strength left to swim and no idea how deep underwater I was, I reached with numb arms, in search of the leg rope connecting me via a band of Velcro around my ankle to my board.

At least the board would float. When finally my fingers closed around the cord, I started to pull myself along it, slowly, with arms that didn't feel connected to my body. Moving along the cord wherever it took me.

Seconds later my head broke the surface and I sucked precious air into my shrivelled lungs. Forcing the dizziness away, I opened my eyes. Just in time to see another swell of dark water. Too slow to close my mouth, I copped another mouthful.

But now my movements were more determined and I clawed for the surface, tipped my head back with lips breaching the surface, desperate for more air. There was no instant relief, but through tunnel vision I managed to pull myself onto the board.

My numb limbs still tingled, but I was far enough out now to be past the breaking waves, and that's where I lay belly-down on the board, regaining strength. Unsure if I was alive, dreaming or had passed over. Nothing felt real. Even the water lacked its usually cool caress.

As soon as I could muster the energy, I paddled further out — far enough to be safe from the pounding waves. It took a long while before I could wiggle fingers and flap legs in an effort to return sensation to them.

With the return of blood flow and oxygen came sharp tingles all over my skin, slowly bringing me back to reality. When I could sit again, I splashed water onto my face, relishing the familiar sensation of cool water over flushed skin.

I was back.

I spotted some people bobbing around out at back of the Bombie and I slowly paddled over to wait for a wave beside them.

'Is that you, Christo? That was one of the worst drillings I've ever seen,' another surfer said as he paddled out later and joined us.

'I got flogged,' I agreed.

> **I wouldn't take anything for granted for a while. Just the security of land alone felt like a blessing.**

'Geez, the sandbank must be bad if you took a hammering. I can't believe you're still going to surf.'

I didn't catch many waves out on the Bombie that day, but it didn't matter. I'd survived and was mighty pleased to get back to shore that afternoon. I knew I wouldn't take anything for granted for a while. Just the security of land alone felt like a blessing. I swore that I would follow my warm-up routines and take the extra minute to put on my vest in the future.

Moments like this helped me realise most problems I previously stressed about day to day were insignificant.

◆ ◆ ◆

The next stop on the world surfing tour was another tropical paradise: the Maldives. An entire country comprising tiny islands scattered across glistening turquoise water, teaming with a rainbow of marine life and coral gardens. The warm air naturally drives you into the tepid water, creating a constant holiday atmosphere. The beauty all around us held no hint of how wrong this trip could go.

After a thirty-minute speedboat journey, Lohifushi Island Resort (since renamed to Hudhuranfushi Surf Resort) was the perfect place to escape the Southern Hemisphere winter and take advantage of the roaring forties blowing offshore all day and the open position in the middle of sea below India to catch swell. Waves in the Maldives were rarely big enough to be dangerous for experienced surfers, so the general mood of competitors was excited and ready for a fun week of high-performance surfing.

Except for those who stayed on boats, everyone else was staying within close proximity of one another — a given considering I could lap the entire island on foot in twenty-five-minutes flat — and the main surf break was conveniently positioned right in front of the resort's many bars. Magic.

I'm not a big eater when I'm on the go all day, but the buffets on the island were enough to turn anyone into a foodie. No kidding, they were the longest tables of luscious food I'd ever seen, with cuisine catering for the varying tastes of international guests.

This is where Jay Moriarity found me one morning in my blue-striped board shorts, staring blankly towards the sometimes overwhelming options of the buffet.

'Hey, dude,' he said. 'You look like you're troubled by a big decision.' He flashed a smile — bright white against his sun-bronzed skin — pale eyes glistening with a sense of purpose beneath short-cropped hair.

'Hell, yeah,' I told him. 'And only so much is going to fit on this plate. Gotta choose wisely.'

He laughed; a deep belly laugh that was typical of his open personality, easily putting people at ease wherever he went.

'It is a bit over the top.' He waved a hand in the direction of the extensive buffet.

'I wonder what happens to the leftover food?' It probably didn't pay to dwell on it, but I sure hoped it was reused or given to staff. I've never been fond of waste. After all, everything we take from the environment has a cost. 'Have you got big plans for the day?'

'Nah, just the usual: a bit of preparation, catch some perfect waves and win the competition.'

'Ha ha! Not if I can help it.'

'The waves might be good to me, dude. It's my birthday on Saturday, so I have to win.'

'Cool. Sounds like an excuse to hit the bars.' I gave him a head nod and loaded some fruit on to my plate.

I could feel a competitive energy on the island. Many surfers were friendly but some were openly not interested in connecting with others, showing that they were there to get the job of competing done. Regardless of how friendly you are, surfing is an individual sport, so we were all there to outdo each other — and sometimes even in the warmest surfs in paradise, tension could develop in the water and aggression could easily escalate.

At lunch I was filling my plate when a Brazilian competitor cut in front of me just as I was about to grab the tongs from the next bayonet. 'Ahhhhgggg.' Instinctively a growling sound came out of me as a subtle way of saying *WTF?* He turned to look at me and we had a silent moment, looking into each other's eyes. *Fuck this guy,* said Bronco. I wanted to save my fight for the competition, but the competition had mentally begun. I didn't want this guy to think he could walk all over me, but I didn't want to start an all-out confrontation. So I gave him my best smile — the one that said, 'I'm gonna kick your ass.' I knew I needed to stick to my pre-event routine, or I would be pissed at myself. Getting caught up in nonsense with someone before the event would be a massive distraction.

Stick to the routine

Over the years, I refined my pre-event routine to include the days prior to the events, as well as the hours. Sure, it took effort to make myself follow this routine, but the results and, most importantly, the peace of mind spoke for themselves. Even when I didn't win, just the belief that the routine was the best way to prepare made me feel like I did all I could.

At times I felt I couldn't be bothered, or self-consciousness kicked in after someone pointed a camera at me while stretching or doing star jumps to warm up. But when I got lazy and didn't stick to the routine, I usually paid the price and hated myself afterwards.

Taking that risk was pointless when I knew what I needed to do.

Mostly the evenings were relaxed affairs with light-hearted discussions over dinner, followed by a few beverages at the bar. It was a great way to end a satisfying day of surfing. On the last Friday of the competition, I was sitting with a bunch of Aussies, finishing off my second plate of food, when one of the Americans from the neighbouring table raised his voice.

'Where's Jay?' The guy had stood up and was bouncing on the balls of his feet, tension rolling off him.

Everyone shrugged their shoulders and he disappeared. Automatically, I scanned the room for Jay's familiar clipped head.

'Hey, apparently the waves will be slightly bigger tomorrow and the winds are looking great,' mentioned a fellow Aussie. We shared a few minutes of conversation about who were the top performers of the day.

Jay's friend returned a short time later, eyes wide, gaze darting around the room.

'Has anyone seen Jay?' he demanded.

'Sorry, but no,' one of the Americans answered. 'Did you check his room?'

'Yeah, I checked his fucking room. Where the fuck is Jay?' His tone cast tension over everyone within earshot.

Conversation in the restaurant lowered to a tense murmur as the Americans frantically came up with a plan to search for the happy-go-lucky Californian.

'It's a tiny island. He couldn't have gone far,' someone said, trying to placate … everyone.

Then everyone started talking over one another. 'He wouldn't miss dinner.' 'Maybe he's on a fishing adventure with one of the locals.' 'He's probably preparing boards for tomorrow.' 'Yeah, no doubt he got carried away with his preparations.' 'His stomach will remind him he's hungry soon enough.'

'Preparations...' Jay's friend said. His face paled and he ran out into the dark.

What the hell was going on? Everyone at the Americans' table rushed off in different directions to search for their friend, retracing his steps since the competition day ended.

My stomach had the weird sensation of dropping to the floor. Jay had been missing long enough for his friends to really worry. An uncharacteristic chill pervaded the restaurant as people stood, wondering what they could do to help. There was an awful feeling of collective uselessness. Whispered voices. Feet shifting uneasily.

'He was diving off the pier this afternoon,' one of the Spanish surfers said, loud enough for many in the subdued restaurant to hear.

'What, you think he's not back from that?' I answered. Pressure built in my ears as though the atmosphere was pressing in on me.

The room was silent, waiting for someone to burst in with good news. They didn't.

I milled about with my fellow surfers, waiting for an update, and recalled a conversation with Jay about using free-diving as part of his training schedule. He loved the profound peace and tranquillity of being submerged without any sounds or equipment distracting him, the satisfaction of mastering his body's reflexes to push past diaphragm spasms, and the sense of accomplishment each time he held his breath a little longer.

'I use the same positive self-talk as I do during big wave surfing,' he'd told me. 'Telling my mind that everything is going to be okay and it doesn't need to panic.'

'I do the same thing,' I'd said. 'But I wonder if lack of oxygen affects our brains. Don't you worry about that?'

'Nah, you get to know your body. I take deep, cleansing breaths before I go under, to build up the oxygen in my blood. And it's not a bad skill to have when you're being hammered under a monster wave.'

Finally news made it back to the restaurant that Jay's backpack had been found at the end of the pier. He had gone free-diving alone. I pushed my plate away, done with food even though there was plenty left. A solid lump formed in my throat as I struggled to process the surreal situation.

Gradually people left the restaurant to walk to the pier. A group of more than fifty people stood in silence. A couple of resort divers arrived in scuba gear and carrying a large, handheld underwater light with handle bars like a bicycle. They dropped off the end of the pier and disappeared into the now black ocean. I stopped halfway along the pier, not wanting to get in the way of rescue efforts and afraid of what I might see.

Mere minutes later there was activity at the end of the pier and the crowd collectively held its breath. A few people started heading for land and I caught the eye of a fellow Australian competitor. I raised my eyebrows in silent question and his face crumpled.

'No good,' he said simply.

I turned and walked back to my villa, feeling like someone had punched me in the guts.

Jay's body was found resting peacefully on a rock ledge, where he'd been perched, holding his breath. Other divers had joined him during the training session, but had come and gone, leaving Jay alone.

A Spanish guy even reported hearing a watch alarm beeping — a sign that its owner should be surfacing. Nobody knew if it had been Jay's watch or if that was the dive he didn't return from, but it was heartbreaking to think someone might have been nearby when he blacked out.

The following day — Jay's twenty-third birthday — the shocked surfing community paid tribute to a fearless man who had faced down some of the biggest and scariest waves on Earth and remained one of the kindest souls on the water. Many small tributes from fellow competitors followed over the next few days and some people left the island, cutting their trip short.

Stay focused — always

When surfing big waves, you're alert for danger, and that includes looking out for other surfers and making sure they surface after a bad wipe-out. But when it comes to training sessions, there's often not the same attention to the risks. No matter your reason for being in the water, a situation can turn dangerous in an instant, and Jay's loss was a lesson for me to be vigilant in my respect for the ocean. The ocean is the boss and she must be respected, even in the most beautiful of times.

News stories and outpourings of grief reverberated around the world after Jay's death. It was a real tragedy that he was taken by a freak accident in calm water, and no doubt each and every surfer on the water was facing their own mortality over the following days, just as I was.

Sure, I'd contemplated having a serious accident while surfing huge waves or over shallow reefs, but it wasn't something I allowed to fester in my mind. There wasn't room in those adrenaline-fuelled situations for negativity. The very reason I worked so hard to keep Bronco at bay was to avoid slipping into a state of paralysing fear when faced with extreme situations.

Many extreme athletes have died doing what they love (and what others view as crazy), but it's always so much more shocking when their final moments come during downtime or training. We're accustomed to seeing them defy death time and time again in the face of imminent danger, and forget how easy it is to let your guard down in commonplace situations, where there isn't an obvious risk. When competing, most professionals will have routines to check all their equipment, get their body and mind into a peak state and be 100 per cent focused. Often during practice we might not follow the routine.

I often thought about the fragility of life after Jay passed away, but I couldn't let it stop me from living mine.

Lessons from the ocean
Routines are magic

In the early years of my business, I spent time reflecting after each important workshop, meeting or event, and kept notes about what did and didn't work. Gradually I refined my routine. This was a practice I had learned from one of the world's top surfers, who gave me some advice when I was only fourteen years old. He said, 'Keep a diary of what you do before each event and each individual heat to prepare, and then write down your results from those events. After some time, you will start to see patterns develop. You will be able to create a preparation routine you know works.'

Now I use preparation routines to prepare for everything, whether it's a surfing competition, business meeting or I just want a productive day. When I permit myself excuses not to follow the routine, I know I haven't committed to doing my best and this leaves me feeling less fulfilled at the end of the day.

Presenting workshops and speaking on stage at business events has generated millions of dollars for my business. This is a high-impact task for me personally, so before I present a workshop, I have a pre-event routine, just like I did when competing. I get up early, do some physical exercise to wake up my brain and body, and get to the venue early so everything is set up before anyone arrives. In those final quiet moments before starting, I like to do a few yoga poses and handstands to get the blood flowing. This puts me in a positive state of mind with energy flowing through my body, and enables me to provide attendees the best of me. Often event organisers will find me stretching with eyes closed before I present a workshop. Bronco will urge me to open my eyes and smile at the person, wanting to be accepted by them, but I battle him in a bid not to be distracted and I remain with eyes closed. I feel the presence of the person looking at me but, exactly like preparing for a surfing event, I know I need to stick to my routine so I don't let anyone else or, most importantly, myself down.

Being present in the moment, knowing I've done all I can to prepare, gives me confidence to show up as my best self for my clients, ready to succeed. Somehow, when I do this, the universe has my back.

Carve your path

♦ If you want to grow your business or career, complete business growth activities and your highest impact tasks like clockwork. To improve your performance, work out how to get yourself into your peak state and the best time of day to do it.

♦ Work out your routine:

1. Set a time every day for important activities—such as marketing and sales activities to generate growth in your business, or your highest impact tasks that make the biggest impact in your career. Commit to this set time so you can work out your routine around a solid foundation. If you allow too many variables, it will be impossible to find your perfect routine, so make time a no-brainer. For example, you could set aside 9 am till 10 am every day to work on marketing activities, and then do your sales calls from 10 am. I use these times as examples because most business owners have more energy at this time of the day, but if that's not you, just find the time that works for you. Most importantly, stick to your committed daily routine and keep in mind this time should be when you have the most energy in the day.

2. Next, start to keep a diary of how you approach the day before 9 am (or whatever your set time is) and what leads you to feeling the most energised to do these growth tasks. It might be ensuring you get a good night's sleep, or perhaps it's doing morning exercise followed by a healthy breakfast—you need to find what works for you. I consulted with a sales team from a luxury motor boat company where the

average sale was over $2 million. I spoke to their top salesperson and found that he did his sales calls at exactly 10 am every day and didn't stop till his calls for the day were done. He believed he wasn't the best salesperson, but he did believe he was more consistent with his approach than others on the team. We rolled out this approach with the rest of the sales team and saw an immediate increase in sales. Remember—sometimes people worry that too much process will kill creativity, but it actually frees so much more time for creativity. Having your processes in place allows you to block out time for creativity and creative thinking.

3. Once you have some data built up in your diary, measure the important numbers—keep track of how many leads and sales you generate, so you're not just basing results on what feels good, but on actual business growth results or outcomes you generate in your role.

4. Finally, review your diary to find what routines generate the best results for yourself, write them down and stick to them.

CHAPTER 7
AFRICA
I've already lost, so I have nothing to lose

Blair and I arrived at a quirky old beachfront hotel in Durban, South Africa, now in our fourth year on the international surfing tour. An armed security guard stood at the front door, which was commonplace here but still took a bit of getting used to for someone from a relatively gun-free country like Australia. Durban is a fun town; always a party going on and new faces to see. Despite the holiday atmosphere, however, an undercurrent of poverty and danger lurked on every corner, with the armed police a constant reminder of this.

As usual, it was peak tourist season and the high prices meant we ended up in cheap, old accommodation. At least it was right on the beachfront with waves to soothe us to sleep, and many of the other competitors were in the same hotel. My quest to make money was being seriously challenged by constantly burning cash while travelling, but luckily the exchange rate to the South African rand was in my favour — and, of course, you can't really put a price on adventure and experience, and I was getting a whole lot of both.

We checked in and promptly opened our board bags, filling the entire room with fiberglass. Now it felt like home. As was our custom, Blair and I then headed straight to the beach for an experimental surf, so we could acclimatise to the local conditions and shake off the all-encompassing numbness in our bodies from an eleven-hour flight. Along the way, I pointed out a restaurant where I'd had a delicious meal the last time I was here, but it was all boarded up.

'What happened to the restaurant?' I asked a local.

He pointed his index finger and raised his thumb in the universal sign of a gun, and then pointed it at me and simulated pulling the trigger. My mouth gaped at the revelation and I was suddenly in a hurry to move on.

It felt so good to have the soothing freshness of ocean after the long trip.

After the surf it was time to hit the streets. Locals had little stalls everywhere, selling all sorts of trinkets, but one item got our attention: plastic toy guns that shot little plastic balls, and were perfect for creating havoc at the hotel. We each bought a gun and hundreds of extra balls.

Back at the hotel, another Aussie waved in the lobby before ducking behind a potted plant and opening fire with a plastic toy gun. It seemed we weren't the only ones with this idea — but he certainly didn't expect us to whip out our own toy guns and fire back!

Innocent guests squealed and ducked out of the way as a shootout ensued, disappearing up the corridor, plastic balls ricocheting off the walls. One guest opened the door to see what the commotion was about and quickly closed it again. Other surfers were drawn by the laughing and yelling and, later that evening, the hotel was full of maniacs with plastic toy guns.

It was awesome fun, although the guns had a bit of a kick and the plastic balls hurtled fast enough to give you a good sting and leave a small, circular welt. As the days progressed, it got to the point where we couldn't leave our rooms without taking our guns to shoot our way out! Some people took to propping their doors open so they could easily fire upon passers-by.

The hotel staff seemed so excited to have international surfers as guests that they laughed at the madness and even assisted with pointing out any potential ambushes we were about to walk into. (Many of the balls were picked up to reload, but we also called a ceasefire each morning, amid feelings of guilt, as the cleaner did his rounds vacuuming up the stray balls.)

They were hilarious (and painful) times, and everyone took to wearing long sleeves — despite the heat — and sunglasses inside, for protection.

◆ ◆ ◆

Durban is a fabulous place to view surfing competitions because the events are held between long piers, enabling spectators to get close to the action with an uninterrupted view. The piers also make for fun waves because they form deep rips next to the pylons, which shape the sand under the water beautifully, consequently shaping nice waves.

During the event, a lot of people were talking about large schools of fish in the area, which usually meant even larger fish following them for an easy meal. The event organisers had a shark-spotting boat out in the water to keep an eye out for schools of fish, although I doubted they'd actually stop a twenty-minute event once it had commenced.

One afternoon I was floating behind the breaks to the side of the competition area, keeping a steady eye out for a good wave, when the water a few hundred metres away came alive. The surface was torn up with frantic fish, splashing and leaping clear of the surface. Their silver bodies glinted and writhed in the sunlight.

Shit! I lifted my feet onto my board.

A frenzied school of fish like this could only mean one thing: predators were hunting them. Several tall fins cut through the centre of the school; they could have been any number of species, but I wasn't sticking around to find out. I started to paddle towards shore even as the alarm sounded and an announcement was made to the competitors in the water.

'All competitors paddle to shore immediately,' the announcer called. 'The event has been put on hold. All competitors paddle to shore immediately for your own safety.'

It wasn't the only time that week events were put on hold due to schools of fish and I wondered just how big the predators chasing them were. But I knew, to disrupt a world-class competition, the shark boat must have seen something big.

◆ ◆ ◆

A night surfing event was rare in competitions, but Durban ran one in conjunction with the main event, so I thought I'd give it a go.

'Why didn't you enter the night event, Blair?'

His blonde eyebrows rose as though the answer went without saying. 'It's scary enough in these waters during the daytime, bro. No fucking way am I going out there at night. It's not like they're going to run the shark boat in the dark.'

I hadn't thought that far ahead, but he was right — running the shark boat would be pointless because it would be impossible to see anything in the black ocean anyway. Of course, Blair came to cheer me on — or possibly see me paddle to my doom.

Just after sunset I got ready for my heat. As I pulled my wetsuit on, my chest tightened, and my breathing became shallow.

What the fuck are you doing this for? Bronco said. *Senseless. There aren't even points for this event and fuck-all prize money. Good chance of dying though.*

I was proper shitting myself by the time I paddled out. *Blair knew it was a shit idea, so why didn't you?*

'Shut up, Bronco,' I snapped into the night. My brother's voice ran through my head. 'All you needed to do is get a couple of good waves, not catch every one. Same goes for trying to do every event and wasting energy on distractions.' He had the condescending tone just right.

I knew this already, so why didn't I act on it? The big points events were what counted if I was going to work smarter not harder. This was a total distraction. And yet here I was, paddling out with three other idiots.

Super bright spotlights were set up along the piers and the beach, aiming intense beams over the water. It sounded like a good solution. In truth, artificial light bounced off the ocean's surface, making the faces of the waves bright silver as they rolled towards the beach, and leaving their

This was a total distraction. And yet here I was, paddling out with three other idiots.

backs with an eerie shadow. I'd surfed in the dark before, but the spotlights produced a strange effect of shadows chasing each wave towards the beach. A tingle ran up my spine and over my shoulders as the impenetrable shadow of a wave passed under me with all the dread of a slow-moving sea monster.

'Well, this sucks,' I mumbled.

The heat got underway, and I spotted a promising wave. Every facet of it glittered in the light shining from behind me, and then I turned to catch it...and was blinded. Shielding my eyes from the wall of light, I was thrown off by the odd perspective, going by feel, unable to see what was ahead of me. I still managed an okay ride and got decent points, but everything felt off kilter.

Do I really care about getting through this heat? It's nothing more than a distraction from the main event. My whole reason for being here. Not one to turn away from a challenge — no matter how foolish — I shook my head, gritted my teeth and paddled back out. Only one more decent ride and I could win this. I had plenty of time remaining.

I took advantage of the rip that formed in the deep channels beside the pier and rode it back out to the breaking waves, gaining a false sense of security close to the brightly lit artificial structure. I say 'false' because there was no way to climb the pillars of the pier in an emergency, and if a surge of water pushed me between the pylons, razor sharp shells would cut me to shreds.

The lights had attracted small sea life to the surface, like a full moon might. Their tiny silver bodies zipped around just below the surface. I ducked under a few breaking waves to get back out past the break, feeling the energy of black water moving around me but disjointed from my surroundings in this unfamiliar world.

This time I didn't go out as far, staying close to the other surfers, figuring it gave me a one in four chance of not being a shark's chew toy. The silver fish were still moving below the surface and each time I caught movement out the corner of my eye, my heart skipped a beat, momentarily unsure if the creature was small or large, friend or foe.

Before long a set of three decent waves came. Three waves and four surfers meant all of the others caught a wave and disappeared out of sight, leaving me out there alone. My blood pressure skyrocketed as I clenched and unclenched my fists to absorb some of the nervous energy coursing through me. The weird perspective of the approaching swells and spooky abyss beneath got my toes tingling.

Bronco kindly reminded me of the feeding frenzies I'd seen during the day. *Those schools of fish are still out there, even if you can't see them.*

When I thought I spotted a big wave coming, I ignored Bronco and paddled further out to meet it ... only to realise it wasn't a wave at all. The strange lighting had tricked me.

You need to get out of here, Bronco urged.

For once, we were in agreement and something close to desperation urged me to return to shore. Why the heck had I paddled out so far? Then, right in front of me, a small fish leapt out of the water.

'Arrgh!'

My entire body stiffened as though an electric shock was coursing through it, so tightly coiled were my nerves. The stupid fish was only a few inches long, but I instantly windmilled my arms, carving water aside to get closer to shore.

On the way in, I caught the first wave that came along, not caring about its scoring potential, only that it was headed in the right direction.

For the remainder of the heat, I caught any wave I could get without going too far out. I've never been so relieved to hear the announcers say I had been eliminated from the rest of the event. And I've never entered another night event.

> **Once all the pressure was gone, I was in top form.**

By the end of the week, Blair and I were both out of the main event. I was hyped up on aggressive energy — angry at myself, for getting distracted by the partying and night events, and for not keeping my head in the game.

Out of the competition, I wandered further down the coast and surfed alone, to blow off some steam, and wouldn't you know it? I performed like a champion. Once all the pressure was gone, I was in top form. This just made me angrier, and I had to breathe through it. If I could relive today, I realised, I wouldn't hold back or let my mind wander. I'd just go for it. Too bad I couldn't have harnessed some of the raw energy surging through me right now.

Come to think of it, I was always wired after losing an event. So, why couldn't I exploit those feelings during my preparation? No reason, so I did.

Flipping visualisation on its head

If I had a dollar for every time someone told me to write my goals down and visualise being on the winner's podium as part of my pre-competition preparation, I would've been a rich teenager. I tried it all—picturing myself doing the right manoeuvres, working smarter not harder, telling myself to forget about sponsor and spectator expectations and just surf.

But none of it worked for me. My goals always seemed really distant and I'd end up daydreaming.

Over the years I made a different kind of visualisation a part of my preparation routine. I closed my eyes and imagined I'd already lost, seethed at the loss, clenched my teeth and fists, and even felt a sinking feeling in my stomach. Then I would tell myself I had one more chance and now was the time to go all in.

This preparation left me fully charged. There was no room for Bronco's negativity or worrying about what other people thought. I would fill with determination and just go for it.

This pain created a far more powerful energy source, which worked for me for years to come. I stayed laser focused on what I needed to do, instead of worrying about everyone else.

Lessons from the ocean
I've already lost, so I have nothing to lose

Visualising the worst-case scenario served me well later in life too. When I was presenting in a business meeting or large keynote presentation and Bronco started chattering, I would think, *What if I had already stuffed this up, how would I feel?* I really tried to visualise and feel the emotions, and then I'd tell myself that I now have been given one more chance to do it properly — so what was I going to do? This made me determined to deliver the highest quality and enjoy it, because this was a bonus opportunity.

Can you use the same approach to help reduce fear when you have an opportunity in front of you? Imagining you have already stuffed up an opportunity or missed it, and then received a second chance, really helps to see the situation as an opportunity and remove fear.

What if you had nothing to lose? Most of the time in business, we don't really lose, we learn. That experience and knowledge continuously makes us better.

You should be calculated in your approach to business and life, but sometimes you need to act on things you really don't have experience in and simply don't know what you're doing, or scare the hell out of you. This is when clear thinking and determination are needed. Try the approach of imagining you've already stuffed it up; really try to visualise it so you feel a knot in your belly. The reality is that if you don't do the thing that's scaring you, you have lost anyway. So you really have lost until you do otherwise.

Public speaking is terrifying for many people and is a good example of when this type of visualisation works well, or even presenting a sales presentation to a small group of people. If you have an opportunity such as this coming up, try the 'I've already lost, so I've got nothing to lose' approach.

Carve your path

- Do you have any big opportunities coming up? Something like a presentation or important meeting? Or maybe something you want, such as asking for a sale, an alliance business to cross promote, a journalist to do a story, an influencer to promote you, or a promotion in your career or new commitments in your role?

- Imagine going through the motions of the important event you've just identified and stuffing it up. How does it feel in your body? Really feel it. At this moment, you haven't really stuffed it up (obviously), but you also haven't done it successfully, so you are at level zero. The only way to go is up. You only have opportunity to gain.

- Now imagine you're being given one more opportunity to make the most of the event you just visualised. Now with nothing to lose, how will you approach it? Go get that damn thing! It's yours!

- Remember that you might need to run through this process again a few minutes before the event. I often do this within twenty minutes of an important event or competition to help silence Bronco.

CHAPTER 8
FRANCE
Where your focus goes, results flow

The second I turned my mobile phone back on, after landing at Biarritz Airport in France, a text message from Mum pinged.

The Billabong team manager has been calling for you. It sounds important.

Weird; he knew I was overseas. Mind you, after a recent loss in California, it couldn't be anything good. Sponsors had been known to cut athletes from their team rather suddenly when they weren't performing, but the timing didn't make sense. I was only just getting started for the year, and I'd had some solid results too.

Billabong's sponsorship money was what got me started in pro surfing and kept me going. They were my main sponsor for fifteen years, and generously provided clothing, surfing accessories and cash, which helped fund my worldwide travels. Sure, I had smaller sponsors who gave me a few thousand dollars here and there for exclusively using their sunglasses, shoes, surfboards or accessories, but without Billabong I was screwed.

Yep, this'll be the end of your surfing career, Bronco chipped in.

I typed a response, although I didn't really want to know the answer.

Me: *What did he say?*

Mum: *Nothing much, but he seemed eager to talk to you. You should call him right away.*

Okay, maybe it wasn't all that bad. He could just want a chat. Yeah right... I ducked into a departure lounge that was empty and pulled out my laptop. I scrolled through the many unread emails until I found one from Bruce at Billabong, the subject line simply reading 'Give me a call'. The actual email wasn't much longer. After hoping I was well, Bruce just repeated his request for me to give him a call, as soon as possible.

Crap! This couldn't be good. Oh well, I better make the most of France and have some fun if it's going to be my last trip. I knew I ought to call Bruce straightaway, but... why face the inevitable and have it spoil my time here? A couple more days couldn't hurt, surely.

While I was on the laptop, I checked my bank account: $1000. And my cash supply was non-existent because my only hope of income in the near future would come from prize money. Usually, prize money would fund around half of my year's expenses, but no wins meant no cash. I desperately needed some good results here on all fronts.

Again, money not making you happy is bullshit — it's easy to say that when you have plenty of it, but when you're staring at a dwindling bank account or peering into an almost empty wallet and wondering if you are going to be able to afford the flight home or meals for the duration of a competition, money can sure feel significant. Of course, money in *itself* doesn't make you happy, but having enough so I didn't have to worry week to week while on tour would certainly equate to a certain degree of happiness. And I knew for sure things would be far easier without cash flow problems.

I *had* to do well in this competition.

Divided values

Money has the capacity to reduce a lot of stress and amplify the good things. After all, being able to pay for dinner out makes me happy. Being able to have an awesome family holiday without worrying about the cost puts a smile on everyone's dial. Stepping into my dream car and knowing it's something I've worked hard for provides an enormous amount of satisfaction. And, nowadays, having money means being able to provide for my family, and spend more time being present with them and making them happy.

The idea of being able to make enough money to never have to worry about it again had been in my mind since I was a skinny-limbed kid catching small waves on the bright yellow boogie board I'd received for Christmas. I always seemed to value money higher than most of my friends. I had always been a good saver, and the idea of work being optional rather than a necessity has always been a long-term goal for me. I always had a sense that I would break through the earning barrier of a regular job and earn enough money to then invest that money so it could continue to make me enough to live happily ever after, at some point. But that belief didn't alleviate the panic of living on the edge of sustainability during my pro surfing days.

(continued)

I now understand that I had divided values. My top values during this time were surfing well (which meant keeping my body in top shape to perform well), living epic experiences while I was funded by my sponsors and then (coming in third) making money. I already knew and believed I could make very good money later in life. I just hadn't yet worked out how, or prioritised it.

Travelling through France was like coming home. The smells and sights of summer — all the greenery and fields of smiling sunflowers tilting their heads towards the light — lit me up inside. The whole energy of a French summer made me feel alive and invigorated.

I decided to put the worry about calling Bruce aside for now and focused on winning.

My base in France was a mate's cabin in the forest near Seignosse, close to the Spanish border in the southwest of France, and just a few minutes' drive to awesome surfing beaches and a couple of cute coastal villages. Laurent had a small one-bedroom cabin hidden in the middle of a forest, in a clearing that was just big enough to kick a ball without it disappearing into the trees.

Three surfing events were being held along the French coast, and the first was a two-hour drive north to Lacanau on the west coast, close to Bordeaux. A friend I had grown up with was a lifeguard on a stretch of coast not far from the Lacanau competition site and invited me to stay with him while competing there. So, I left a bunch of my things in the cabin and took off solo in my hire car.

The French were out in droves, enjoying summer holidays along the coast and lining the wide, flat beaches. It was commonplace for beachgoers to be barely dressed or even naked, which took a bit of getting used to for this Aussie guy. The ocean was lovely and warm, and the best part was that it didn't get dark until 10 pm, so we had plenty of hours for surfing each day. We'd often have dinner and then head out for another surf around 8.30 pm, when the crowds had disappeared.

After checking the competition site and schedule, I drove out of town towards the location my friend Sean had given me to find his accommodation. As I headed out of town, I noticed a lot of forest with not much else around, which would make for a quiet, secluded holiday spot. A single-lane road wound through the trees, further and further from any sign of civilisation, and I started to worry what sort of accommodation it would be.

Finally, through a gap in the trees, I spotted people playing golf. Hang on a minute — I did a double take — they were naked. Four people stood around a green, all focused on the one who was concentrating on putting, and they were starkers apart from shoes and a golf glove. A nervous chuckle bubbled up from my throat.

I arrived in the resort parking area and read the signage. There had been no mention of a nudist colony when my mate had invited me. I hoped they wouldn't expect me to walk around naked. The property was protected by a boom gate, so I headed on foot to the reception area.

Naked holidaymakers were everywhere: riding bicycles, holding hands, mums and dads playing ball with their children, all going about their days as usual and all totally naked. Approaching the reception office, I could see lily-white bottoms lined up at the counter as guests asked questions.

It was all too much, and I started giggling.

Desperately, I tried to pull myself together, but the giggles wouldn't be suppressed, and people were glancing my way. I backed away. Once I was at the boom gate, I turned and speed-walked back to my car, leaping in and locking the door as an uncontrollable case of the giggles struck me. The image of Sean strutting around in his birthday suit as he worked here just made it worse.

I scooched down in the seat in a poor attempt to hide. Clenching my jaw and pressing my lips together only ended in spluttering as I laughed harder, jaw aching from the strain. Tears streamed down my cheeks, and I gulped desperate breaths of air as my chest constricted.

A sweat broke on my brow in the stifling car. This was ridiculous. If anyone saw me, it would look so bad. Still, the more I tried to stop, the funnier it all seemed and the harder I laughed. Pretty soon a security guard would be sent to ask me to leave.

Finally, Bronco piped in with a voice of reason (now there was an irony). *You can't just sit in a car outside a nudist colony laughing,* he warned. *This screams pervert. You either need to get a grip or drive away.*

But if I left, it would be so much harder to return, and Sean was expecting me.

It was a full ten minutes before I managed to rein in the hysterics, fan my red face and breathe normally.

With my game face on, I headed back to the reception office. Thankfully, the staff were dressed in a uniform. They directed me to Sean's cabin and gave me a gate pass. The vastness of the resort became evident as I drove, with different types of accommodation available from hotels and holiday cabins to camping. There was a post office, a supermarket, several restaurants and all sorts of sports activities and amenities, including multiple swimming pools, tennis courts, a golf course, mini-golf and cycling. Impressive.

I dumped my stuff in Sean's cabin and pondered whether I was expected to strip off. Nah, I decided I'd wait and see what Sean said. In the meantime, I ditched the T-shirt and kept my shorts (a good compromise) and headed out to find him.

The beach where Sean would be lifeguarding was supposed to be just over the sand dunes. Because it was late afternoon, almost everyone was leaving the beach, so I was walking against a steady stream of naked people — seriously, hundreds of nudists coming right at me. The only thing I can liken it to was going against the flow of a festival crowd. I had to weave between them, trying not to bump into anyone, and averting my gaze so I wouldn't look like a pervert, although I did notice that quite a few should have applied sunscreen more liberally on places that weren't used to sun exposure.

Being the only one wearing clothes felt super weird and made me self-conscious about my board shorts — not enough to make me strip off, but I did wonder what everyone was thinking about the odd one out. Perhaps they thought I was covering up a problem or something.

When I finally crested the last sand dune and saw the expanse of beach before me, I immediately felt at home, despite the odd individual still frolicking naked by the water.

It was a relief when I eventually found Sean on a lifeguard tower. You guessed it, he was naked, but at least he had a towel loosely wrapped around his waist for a little cover. The other lifeguards had nothing on at all, which begs the question — how did people actually identify who was a lifeguard?

◆ ◆ ◆

Staying at the nudist colony was quite the experience, and my first few conversations with nude guests were difficult. I became aware of my peripheral vision like never before. For some reason, it was most awkward with males. Like the guy who stopped me to ask how my trip was going and where in Australia I was from. It's not like I could miss his penis just dangling there. My mind was all over the place and I struggled to get through the conversation. And the beach was always busy, so everywhere I turned were more penises, boobs or vulvas staring back at me.

On the third day, I finally felt like I was getting into the groove of hanging out with nudists, so I bravely grabbed my surfboard, draped a towel and shorts over it (I still felt like I needed clothing with me, even though I wasn't wearing it), and peered out of the cabin.

The coast was clear, so I took a deep breath and walked out naked. A refreshing breeze flowed around parts that were usually sheathed. On the way to the beach, tourists greeted me and went about their activities without a sideways glance.

On the beach, I found a patch of sand to myself and spread out my towel. Surfing nude was excellent; freeing. I didn't want to burn any delicate parts, but it felt too weird to apply sunscreen to my privates, so instead I kept the surfs short.

While sitting on the beach, I watched a family playing with a bat and ball. Mum, dad, a teenage son and daughter. They were all laughing and enjoying themselves — naked. In Australia, a teenager wouldn't be caught dead naked in front of their family or friends, and it made me wonder about the self-consciousness that was trained into us. It seemed so ordinary at the resort, but I still couldn't quite get used to it while I was there. Perhaps it was just a matter of more time needed for me to fully relax.

Ludicrous as it may seem, at dinnertime guests dressed up elegantly, with makeup on and hair coiffed to attend the nicer restaurants. But often a few diners hadn't made it home to change after their daytime activities. Occasionally, someone would stand and walk across the restaurant with nothing on but a T-shirt for a little warmth. No-one batted an eyelid.

Sean seemed comfortable with the whole situation, but whenever we met, we both opted to wrap a towel around ourselves to avoid any uncomfortable situations. Of course, it was my own insecurities that made me uncomfortable, but it's difficult to undo a lifetime of conditioning.

◆ ◆ ◆

The endless sandy beaches around the Lacanau event were alive with holidaymakers and enthusiastic spectators. The upbeat mood was infectious and flowed through to my competition preparation activities, and then onto the waves.

Some days everything just feels right. The sun is shining, the water glistening, your brain is switched on and full of positive thoughts. This was how it was during this event. Every time I stood on my board, the harmony between body, brain and environment had me performing with ease, feeling like my board was an extension of my body, performing complicated manoeuvres and enjoying the process.

> **It was my own insecurities that made me uncomfortable, but it's difficult to undo a lifetime of conditioning.**

After a fantastic result in a highly rated event, French beachgoers came up to chat. Thankfully, these ones were all clothed, but I was also struck by how many of them were wearing Billabong clothing.

Everyone who was anyone was wearing surf-brand clothing, no matter if they looked like it was really their first time at the beach. I guess it wasn't surprising that so much of it was Billabong branded, even this far from Australia. Billabong had come a long way from the two warehouses they had in different locations when they first started sponsoring me, to a giant complex so vast the leadership team used skateboards to get around inside. They also had a giant retail store on the Gold Coast on its very own street: Billabong Place. It was a good time for surf brands, and a good time to be sponsored by a big one doing well.

It was a timely reminder that I needed to get up the nerve to call Bruce back. After all, Billabong was my major sponsor and their contract was more than fair. All they asked of me was to exclusively wear their clothes and have a sticker in the top thirty centimetres of all my surfboards. Pretty simple, really.

But a small conflict was going on inside me. On the one hand, Billabong was a rich company; on the other hand, I routinely worried they would cut me off.

I built up my courage and used a roadside payphone to avoid high fees on my mobile. The conversation went something like the following:

'Hey Bruce, it's Christo.'

'Christooo, how are ya, buddy?'

Okay, he was acting way too nice. Bruce was usually very friendly, but busy, so he would cut straight to the point very quickly. A very direct, no fluff kind of guy. The last time I saw him talk in this overly enthusiastic way to another Billabong member, the guy had just won a world title. Little old me didn't usually get this kind of charm, which made me suspect this was also his 'we're breaking up' tone.

Keen to delay the inevitable, I continued with small talk. 'I'm good Bruce, a bit jet-lagged. I'm in France, just had a surf and it's super-hot here.' Maybe he'd buy that jet lag was why I'd taken so long to call back.

'How's the surf?' he asked.

'Small but the water's warm, which is awesome. Nice to be out of a wetsuit.'

The small talk ran its course and I held my breath waiting for Bruce to get to the point.

'Buddeeeee.' My stomach dropped to my feet. 'Have you seen the story in *Waves Magazine*?'

Waves was one of the top surfing magazines in Australia and Billabong spent tens of thousands of dollars advertising in it every month.

'Nah, missed it while travelling. What's going on?' I wasn't sure where this was leading.

'The story about your Indonesian trip has been published and you got more photos than anyone else. Including two full double-page spreads! We're stoked. You're a legend around here.'

I remembered the photo shoot Bruce was talking about, back in Indonesia. With the machinations of magazine publishing, the story had only just come out.

'I wanted to say well done from the team, champ. This brings so much value to us as a brand. There's cash for your photo bonuses on its way too, and if you need anything else at all, just go into the Billabong office there in France. Anything at all, mate. Make the most of their support.'

A fly buzzed past my gaping mouth, and I snapped it shut, blinking as I processed his words. They were stoked with me. *Not* cutting me from the team.

> **They were stoked with me. *Not* cutting me from the team.**

We ended the call and I kind of deflated in a relieved pile. I still had my sponsor and they were happy with me.

After the Lacanau event, Billabong increased my level of sponsorship and sent me on several photographic trips for various surf magazines. It was perfect timing to help me progress to doing more of the world tour events.

An idea had also lodged in my brain. What if I could fund the rest of my surfing career just by consistently getting photos published in magazines? It was a tactic that had been staring me in the face, but I'd never seriously considered it before. Now, I started to imagine how much weight it would take off my shoulders, not to mention preserving my value to Billabong.

As I continued to think the possibilities through, a new plan started to form. The same would be true for other brands, so I had the potential to get more sponsors, enough to see me through the whole year (as long as I didn't go against any existing agreements). I'd made friends with plenty of surfing photographers over the years, and they were always looking for good surfers to shoot. This became an approach that served me well for many years.

Harnessing opportunities

In life and business, a million different opportunities are always ready to pull me in different directions, and it's never easy to choose which one to take advantage of. I need to clearly know what I value most to direct my attention. Many opportunities are mere distractions from my purpose. As a professional surfer, my purpose is clear: win the next event! Simple. In business, mini 'events' are occurring constantly. Every sale is like a mini event, every opportunity is a mini event.

Through years of experience, I am now able to harness the emotional charge of energy that comes from the uncertainty of not knowing what's next, and channel it into productivity. I do high-impact work based on my top priorities when I have the most energy in the day, and believe the ability to stay ruthlessly focused on what I believe to be the biggest opportunities for business growth, no matter the external distractions or personal insecurities, is the main reason I've gone on to generate millions of dollars in my businesses over the years. I value business growth higher than most people I know, so I have grown more.

In surfing competitions, you see amazing waves come straight to your competitors and you get good at staring the challenge in the face. You really need to know your plan of attack and be open to change, but at the same time you can't get distracted from the real reason you're there. My ego would sometimes get in the way, making me want to do an impressive manoeuvre to impress the crowd, when really it was safer to just complete a wave, get the score I needed

(continued)

and simply get through the heat because winning was all that mattered. This was a very clear priority.

In business, ego is often a problem for many people too. This is another reason you really need to be clear on your top values, and know what is most important to you and your brand. This will help you get out of your own way when maybe someone has a different idea to you, or someone else becomes the face of your brand, or someone else leads a meeting — or whatever else challenges your ego. If you can see it serves your highest values, you can bite your lip and go with their idea.

Lessons from the ocean
Where your focus goes, results flow

When working with business owners with my business, we get clear on their company values. These are basically a set of non-negotiables the company operates by and prioritises how they operate — for example, customer service, innovation, leadership, fun, generosity or any number of descriptive words. However, to take things further, we also need to look at ourselves in the same way. We all operate by a set of values and whatever we value highest gets the most of our attention, and the most results. If you value your relationship higher than making money, for example, you will stop work to spend time with your partner. If it's the other way around, your relationship might struggle because you're always working to make more.

A client I was mentoring for a couple of years came to my office for an initial meeting. He owned a website development and online marketing company. My team met him and we asked him what he wanted as a result of working with us. He clearly said, 'I want to make more money. I've been in business a long time and I'm tired of barely covering costs.' So, as a priority, we got underway with implementing growth strategies in his business.

Over the course of a year, his business went from strength to strength. He employed new team members and was making more money than ever before — and this is where it gets interesting. He shared with me that by taking care of his highest value at that point in time — that is, to *make more money* — he could now focus on other values. He also wanted to get heathier and look after himself more, and improve his relationship and family life. With the new marketing systems in place, he could now work the equivalent of a four-day week and shift his values. We continued to assist with improving the business growth strategies, and within another six months—just eighteen months after starting work with us—he came back into my office to see me. Two of my employees came and told me an 'attractive guy' was asking for me. I peeked into the waiting area and told them who he was—while they remembered him, they were in total shock that it was the same person. He was a transformed person, and the confidence he now carried was magnetic.

Trying to juggle too many values might leave you doing mediocre in many areas. We each usually only do three values really well; however, we can change them. You're in control of you! For example, if your top values are making money, your health and time with friends, your relationship will likely struggle. If your top values are education, your relationship and travel, you'll not likely be saving much money. You'll be good at whatever you value the most.

Early in my surfing career, my highest values were competitions, health and adventures; however, as I wrapped up full-time surfing, making money moved up the priorities list and, later in life, my family has become my highest value.

Often people tell me they're not good at something, but this isn't quite correct. It's simply a matter of their values. If you want to get better at something, associate it with one of your highest values—for example, if I wanted to focus and feel motivated to make more money, I could connect all the benefits more money would have on my family life. I could make a list of the benefits my family would gain with more money, including all the experiences, toys, a nicer home and reduced financial stress.

As I write this, my top three values are family, health and surfing/fun, so my day is built around those values. I surf every morning, my team know I don't take meetings before 10 am or after 4 pm, or on weekends—afternoons and weekends are for family time. Valuing surfing also means I want to surf in the best locations on Earth, so this also means my business needs to run while I'm surfing and I need to be able to run it from anywhere on Earth. (Fun fact: I'm in Bali right now for two weeks as I write this part of this book. My days while here start with family fun first thing in the morning, then surfing with my partner, then a little work, surfing again after lunch and then family play time again in the afternoon.)

Carve your path

- Have a think about what you value the most in your life right now (even if it's playing video games). Make a list and prioritise the top values in order of most to least. Having a long list is okay, but finalise the top three in order of priority. You might already start to gain some insights into your results in different areas of life, just by doing this first step.

- In what areas of life do you want to improve? Write them down. Can you create connections between your existing values with the areas you want to improve in life? For example, if you want to learn more but your highest priority is making money, think about what you can learn that will increase your income. Maybe you want to prioritise family — can you bring your family into parts of your business, so you get more time with them.

- Considering what you want to improve, can you spot any new values you would like to prioritise? Write down any new order of priority if needed.

CHAPTER 9

SPAIN AND PORTUGAL

Done is better than perfect

The biggest of the French events was held at Hossegor beach, in big surf with strong currents. I was coming off a high from previous events, had a stash of US dollars from prize money in a sock in my travel bag (and more money on the way from Billabong), which validated me and my potential. The general euphoria of being in France felt good.

The sandbanks at Hossegor were split so waves were breaking a long way out as well as closer to shore, with a deep channel in between. So, I had to decide where to position myself before each round. I watched the waves closely each morning, trying to get an idea of where they were breaking most consistently. My planning paid off, with a good run of heats as I progressed steadily through the event over the week.

Of course, each day, the shape of the sandbanks changed and big tides moved the waves to different sections of the sandbanks. This meant the wave quality and pattern of the waves changed too, making planning tricky. One day, I misjudged a wave and had a massive wipe-out, hitting a sandbank under the water, hard. I was left sporting a large bruise across one thigh and scratches all over my leg.

Three-time world surfing champion Tom Curren (winning in 1985, 1986 and 1990) was also competing in this event. He was smooth as silk when he glided along each wave and somehow looked like he never aged. So innate was his talent that it seemed like he saw the waves differently to everyone else, and like the ocean was an extension of his body. I was honoured to be sharing waves with one of my heroes. This was a man who was at the top of his game when I was a toddler, and yet he still beat me in one of the heats.

With three days remaining in the competition, most of my friends had been eliminated, so it was party time for them. Not for me, though — I needed to remain focused.

In my final heats, a good wave came through in the last couple of minutes. I looked at it, and part of me knew this wave could get me through the heat, but Bronco chimed in. *What if there's a better wave behind it?*

Uncertain, I paddled into position to catch the wave. As I was drawn up the swell, I scanned the green face of the wave, attempting to predict its scoring potential. Waves usually come in sets of several waves, each wave in the set larger than the last was the pattern that day, so I backed off, sure a better wave would be right behind it.

Once I dropped over the crest of the wave, however, a flat ocean stretched out behind it.

'Fuck! Shit, shit, shit.'

That single moment of indecision and wanting more, rather than just getting the job done with what was in front of me, was enough to eliminate me from the competition.

Losing is swift and final. That's it, you're out. No changing it. No more chances. Go pack your things and say goodbye. Some might see it as bad luck. To me, it was a missed opportunity that would haunt me for years — a split-second decision that I got wrong.

Hot fury burned through me and I jogged up the beach with tunnel vision. Not wanting to stop and chat to other competitors or fans, desperate to disappear

Losing is swift and final.

under the crushing weight of frustration. I returned my coloured vest and headed straight for the car, no idea of where I was headed, just needing to be somewhere else.

Imperfect action versus inaction

Hindsight's a bitch. Looking back, it's easy to see how to win an event, but in the moment you make decisions based on myriad factors, including wave conditions, time remaining, the energy flowing through your body and your reading of the water. My strength and surfing technique were great that day. I knew I could win. But a split-second decision cost me the prize, and the French leg of the surfing tour was over for me.

A colleague who has studied human behaviour and works with people on their mindset told me, 'The mind is like Velcro for negative things that happen in our lives, and like Teflon

(continued)

for the good things.' An understanding of this would have been handy in my early days of competing.

I would lie in bed thinking about that moment for years to come; to this day, the thought of it makes me anxious and occasionally wakes me from a dead sleep. But it did teach me a valuable lesson. Imperfect action is always better than inaction or procrastinating in the hope of something better being just around the corner.

Missing a wave or procrastinating about a task can have the same effect on success, whether it's a surfing event or business. The ability to take action without overthinking has been key to the success of business owners I have mentored.

When I feel myself going down the path of overthinking a situation, or procrastinating about what to do next, I always start at the top of my 'to-do' list and work on the highest-impact task first. I ruthlessly focus and ignore everything else.

One of my business team members recently said to me, 'You never procrastinate.' This surprised me at first, but after considering how I work and being taken back to that moment in a wave in Hossegor, I can see why. During certain moments in business, I know I need to act. The outcome might not be obvious, but every task moves me forwards. Every decision is an opportunity not to be missed. Just make the best decision in the moment based on what's in front of you and get moving; don't wait for perfection or the next best thing (or wave).

Hundreds of business owners I have worked with struggle with their own worst enemy, their own Bronco. Overthinking and not acting.

The next stop on the world surfing tour was a nice stretch of beach in the small city of Zarautz, Spain, a mere thirty-minute drive from the French border.

Zarautz Beach has a small bay with a narrow beach, protected at either end by headlands. The sun rose over one headland and set over the other, so it wasn't glaring in my eyes during early and late surfs. A paved promenade, raised above the beach, ran along the western half of the bay, topped by two historical octagonal rotundas with ornate balustrades in the centre of the beach, where tourists could look out over the water.

Unfortunately, Mother Nature did not focus her energy on creating quality waves during this event and the swell was minimal. The dates were set, so we were forced to compete anyway, which left an awful lot to luck. Waves never offer an even playing field, even in the best conditions, but the better quality they are, the more scoring potential they have.

I noticed a lot of negative talk among the competitors about the poor conditions. 'Everyone's in the same boat. Need to get the job done, even if the scores aren't perfect,' I mumbled to myself as a mini pep talk.

Simon — my surfboard shaper — had recently made me a board for small waves. It had a layer of lighter than usual thin fiberglass over the foam core to reduce weight. This made it more delicate, but also

Get the job done, even if the scores aren't perfect.

more responsive to fast turns and faster on tiny waves. With it in my kit, I felt ready.

Blair picked up this new board, studied it and frowned. 'It's very light, but it looks exactly the same as those three, bro.' He waved a hand in the direction of the pile of boards I'd packed for this trip.

'Ah,' I said. 'But it's completely different in the water. This one,' I picked up an almost identical-looking board 'is heavier and I don't like it unless the waves are big.'

Since a young age, surfboards had become an extension of my body. I no longer felt the board under my feet; rather, I sensed the water with the edges of the board, like my mind was inside the fibreglass. As I focused on where to go, we moved as one, gliding through the water. So, the slightest difference in weight had made the new board come to life. It was more manoeuvrable and more responsive.

◆ ◆ ◆

Even with the right equipment, I only secured a mid-level result in the event, so I jumped in the car with four others for a full-day drive across Spain and into Portugal, with many changes of the designated driver due to us all being so tired and some also being hungover. The car was a mid-sized hatchback, and I counted thirty surfboards strapped to its roof.

With five surfers and a giant board bag each, the height of the boards on the roof was as much as the car itself. The bags were 'secured' with tie-down straps looped right over the boards, through the inside of the car and then pulled tight, with the latch inside the car. I doubted we would make it without a drama. But, we did eventually make it safely to Praia Grande, Portugal, had a week there, followed by another ten-hour drive back to Pantín, Spain, for an event. After all that, I was feeling exhausted.

I stayed with some fellow competitor friends a twenty-minute drive out of Pantín, in a lovely holiday rental surrounded by farmland and an orchard. A variety of fruit trees were heavy with ripe, summer fruit, so I picked an armful and sat on the grass to eat, basking in the serenity of being immersed in nature. After the madness of Portugal, it was nice to be in such a secluded, peaceful location.

One afternoon I was hanging around the house after a day of surfing, thoroughly enjoying a quiet afternoon alone after constantly being with people for months.

A surfing friend, Chris, messaged. The text conversation went something like the following:

Chris: *Hey, buddy, the event organisers are putting on free drinks and platters of mussels. I didn't want you to miss out.*

Me: *Thanks mate, but I'm all good just hanging.*

Chris: *There's going to be a special announcement too. I'm on my way to pick you up.*

Not sure if he had even read my reply, I didn't protest. Clearly, he was already buzzed from having a few of those free drinks.

I wandered outside to wait for my ride, hosing down the new surfboard I'd used earlier and leaving it on the concrete footpath to dry. Then I sat on the porch, soaking up the sun, letting my heavy eyelids droop. I wasn't sure I could be bothered going out at all.

My eyes popped open at the sound of a car approaching.

Chris waved as he sped up the driveway and grinned when he spotted the mud puddle the front yard had become after some heavy rain. Full of bravado, he turned the car into a side slide as he hit the mud. I was fairly sure he was picturing a James Bond–type move where he'd slide across the yard and skid to a perfect stop by the front door. Well, it was an elegant start…

The car slid sideways across the yard, coming in hot. It overshot the muddy grass with no sign of slowing and hit the high lip of the footpath that wrapped around the house. For a breath-holding moment the vehicle became airborne, bounced onto the path and skidded across my new surfboard, coming to rest inches from the house.

I would forever be grateful for the height of that footpath, which slowed the momentum of the car. Without it, Chris would have punched a dirty great hole in the side of the house. The house survived; pity the same couldn't be said for my board. Once Chris had reversed off the path and bounded out of the car, we inspected the damage.

'Oh shit, sorry buddy.' Chris grimaced.

The once glossy, unmarked board now had deep, muddy tread marks depressed into the length of it. It was no more than an ornament now, and its destruction kind of felt like an omen. Perhaps it was signalling the end of my surfing career. After all, Portugal was a disaster and I hadn't had any amazing results at the last few events. Now my newest board was destroyed.

Time to go home, whispered Bronco.

I tended to agree with him. I decided I'd stay the week to finish this event and just strip things back to purely focus on my best tricks while surfing — no pressure, enjoy it and then fly home. I just needed to do the best with whatever comes my way.

> **I just needed to do the best with whatever comes my way.**

Billabong would be shocked, but my family would support my decision to end my professional surfing career. A bunch of ideas for business ventures had been floating about my head, so I could focus on them.

Chris apologised all the way back to the beach, so I couldn't stay angry, but the melancholy lingered. I'd had a lot of fun over the years but always knew it would end someday.

While we enjoyed some relaxed drinks and local seafood, the event organisers gathered everyone around for an announcement.

'We will be running an extra team event as well as an individual specialty event for the best single aerial manoeuvre.'

Chris elbowed me. 'What do you think?'

'Yeah, why not? I'm in.' It's not like I had anything to lose at this point. May as well put my name down for both events and have a bit of fun.

The next morning, I parked the muddy hire car in the fan-shaped esplanade car park and lugged my board along the walkway that crossed the sloping grass to the sand. The sky was clear and sets of decent-sized waves rolled towards shore. My spirits lifted.

Groupings for the team event were predetermined by country of origin. Overall, my group of Aussies came second and pocketed a few hundred dollars each in prize money.

The aerial event was held later in the day and thirty competitors were all sent into the surf at once. The small cove was crowded, making it extra difficult to fight your way onto a good wave.

An aerial competition was new to me and how to win one was a mystery. My brother Nick's voice ran through my mind. 'You only need two good waves to win.' It was one of his favourite sayings when I was a kid, but this time it all came down to a single aerial manoeuvre within the allotted time. No other tricks would count towards winning at all.

I managed to catch a wave and complete a small aerial manoeuvre that was nothing special. I was paddling back out when a good mid-sized wave reared up. A few people started paddling, but were too far out to really have a chance. It raced towards me. Being on my front side with my face to the wave was a great position to do a good aerial manoeuvre. 'This is the one,' I told myself.

Get going, Bronco snapped.

So, I swung my board, and tore at the water with my hands to generate paddle speed to give me a smooth entry into the wave and enough speed for a manoeuvre. Jumping up to plant my feet in the centre of the board, I pushed the board hard across the steep face of the wave, gaining plenty of speed. Just as the crest of the wave started to pitch, I launched off the lip.

The board flew into the air a few feet before landing smoothly on the top of the breaking wave and gliding over the lip onto the flat water in front of the now broken wash of the wave. The familiar thrill of job well done coursed through my veins, although it was impossible to know how everyone else had performed with so many on the water. With any luck the water would go flat for the remaining thirty-five minutes and no-one else would get such a great opportunity.

◆ ◆ ◆

By the end of the week, I had secured a semi-final finish in the main event, which gave me a few thousand dollars in cash and did wonders to renew my confidence. A big crowd of enthusiastic Spanish were at the presentations and the winners from the teams event had elected an eccentric adopted Aussie by the name of Wayne 'Shiva' Glasscock to go on stage to collect their trophy.

He was a Texan who had learnt to surf in Hawaii (at the age of twenty-four), and then moved to Australia, deciding to surf in the world series when he was thirty-six. When I chatted with him, he said he owned a tea-tree farm. He battled on the surfing tour for four years with nothing but poor results. He surfed in around a dozen competitions per year, staying illegally in a tent on most competition beaches. The only event where I ever saw him progress through a heat was in Portugal, and only after two of the other surfers didn't show up. Shiva Wayne made his way onto the stage to collect the trophy. Making the most of this glorious moment in his career, he proceeded to make a speech.

During the speech, prankster Matt Bemrose had snuck around the back of the stage. He appeared behind Shiva, pulling the man's tracksuit pants down, undies and all. So, there was Shiva, standing on an elevated stage, facing directly into the afternoon sun half naked, for hundreds of people to view.

Shiva wasn't going to relinquish the moment, so he just kept on clutching the microphone in one hand, while struggling to tug his pants up with the other.

The crowd erupted into laughter. I battled between doubling over with tears streaming down my face and watching poor Shiva act as though it was all part of the show while he attempted to right the wrong. He deserved another medal for being such a good sport and taking it all in his stride.

I was still swiping moisture from my eyes and grinning like a loon when the results of the aerial contest were announced. Fifth, fourth and third place getters were announced.

'Bummer, it would've been good to get a placing,' I mumbled to Chris, a bit pissed off considering I felt as though I'd done well.

Second place was called. 'And the winner of the aerial event is Christo Hall from Australia,' the announcer called.

Applause exploded through the crowd. Heads turned left and right, searching for him. For a moment I was stunned, like a kangaroo caught in headlights. Then people shoved me towards the stage. I was miles back, which made for an awkward journey, pushing my way through the sea of bodies as people clapped me on the back.

I finally climbed up to the stage. 'Bring it on; I'm back, baby!'

Lessons from the ocean
Done is better than perfect

Many business owners overthink things. We're faced with so many options for just about anything—from which software to use for video hosting and email marketing, to which website hosting to use. Often, simply making a decision and acting is the most important thing.

I recently worked with two separate yoga studio owners and had an initial consult separately with each. Funnily enough, they both didn't have software in place to manage their customer database and email marketing, and were both doing lot of manual work. I explained this work could be automated to free up time they could use to continue to grow their customer base.

The first client got straight onto the software I recommended and signed up as soon as I stood up from our meeting. The second client wrote down my recommendation and added a note to her 'to-do' list to check it out and research other options.

A month later, I had a strategy call with both clients. When I spoke to the first client, she told me she was over the moon with her new systems—she had automated her online registrations, follow-up emails, SMS reminders, 'refer a friend' emails and review request emails, *and* had a monthly newsletter-type email already scheduled for next month. She was making more sales than ever and had put managing her customer relationships on autopilot.

When I spoke to the second client, she said she had been busy and was still planning to check out some different software. She had spoken to a friend who suggested a different option, and at a business networking event another yoga teacher mentioned what they used. Her results were a longer 'to-do' list.

The client who was getting the best results from her actions was clear.

I also apply this same approach to my own business. At times, I've received negative feedback when someone has found a few spelling mistakes in my writing. I'll be honest: I'm not a natural writer—despite the evidence in your hands to the contrary! My mind was out the window most of the time in English class, and all I thought about was what the surf might be like.

I worked with a very successful owner of eleven real estate agent franchises, and at one of our meetings he told me he had found a spelling mistake in a folder I had provided as a resource to him and his team. I told him that folder had made me millions of dollars as a valuable resource, and no-one had ever mentioned the typo before. He gave me a warm smile, told me to 'Leave the spelling mistake as it is, then' and laughed.

If I had waited to do everything perfectly, I don't think I would have completed anything.

Carve your path

◆ Is there something you're working on at the moment that you're struggling to get right? Or maybe you're overthinking how to get started rather than just starting?

◆ Keep it in mind that imperfect action will always beat no action. If you know your values and operate with integrity, people will forgive you for a stuff-up once in a while — but the returns on action will be infinitely higher than those from inaction. What do you need to act on right now to make a happier you?

CHAPTER 10
KANGAROO AND CANARY ISLANDS

Your beliefs about yourself are BS

I stood at the top of a cliff on Kangaroo Island, South Australia, and looked down at a writhing fur seal colony. Grey, slug-like bodies lounged on rust- and black-coloured granite slabs above the pounding surf of the Southern Ocean, occasionally diving headfirst into the fluid abyss.

'Surf looks good,' I said to my buddies, as though that outweighed the potential for death.

We'd just endured a tiring hour-long hike along a barely there bush trail to this remote location, so there was no way I was leaving without at least *attempting* a surf — shark-infested waters or not.

'They didn't say we'd be surfing beside a seal colony.' My mate sounded sceptical but didn't voice what we were all thinking. Seals were a shark's favourite snack, and we would be floating in the same water. I rolled my tongue around a suddenly dry mouth.

Each of us not wanting to be the first one to shy away from danger, we made the climb down the cliff face to the slippery rocks below. I picked a path to the edge of the rock ledge, where the pitted surface gave the soles of the feet a little pinch. Then I spent a few minutes learning the rhythm of the waves. When I was ready (as I'd ever be), I waited for the next wave to approach. Three quick breaths out and I launched myself and board into the air, over the wave's crest, landing flat on the board and paddling like hell to get clear of the waves smashing against the rocks.

Sitting on the board in the ink-black water, an instinctive need for self-preservation kicked in and I pulled my feet up and rested them on the board, imagining jagged-toothed monsters watching from the dark depths.

Well, there isn't any point in staying still and being an easy snack for the sharks, Bronco urged.

He had a point, so I reminded myself that this rising panic was nothing more than the curse of the fight or flight response; my brain's innate self-protection strategy, which erred on the side of safety, sending signals to flee at the first sign of potential danger.

So, I fought through the thrill of terror-induced adrenaline pumping through my veins and the little flip of nervous anticipation in my gut. With one eye scanning the approaching swell and the other searching the water for moving shadows, I caught the next wave.

Once I got into a rhythm, the nerves subsided and the joy of flying across the water with agile seals pirouetting all around me outweighed the fear.

Overriding fear

Of course, fear is a good thing...when the danger is real. But if I let my body's natural reaction to nerves rule my life, I would never try anything new. Brains are clever, but they're no match for emotions. The sensations and physical reactions I feel are the same whether I'm about to paddle out at a surfing competition, make a difficult decision, step onto a stage in front of a crowd, get into an argument or leap into shark-infested waters.

Unfortunately, our brains can't distinguish between excitement and danger; our body's reaction is the same whether the threat is real or perceived.

Reacting to the initial message to flee when we experience a potentially dangerous situation is instinctual — totally out of our control. I could be sitting on my board, waiting for the right wave, and if a dolphin suddenly broke the surface right beside me or swam right under me, my first thought would be that a monster was about to bite me. The shock would send my heart racing, stomach flipping and muscles tensing, ready to flee, all before I'd even taken a breath. Then, the logical part of my brain would engage and I'd realise it was just a friendly mammal coming for a closer look.

If I'd surrendered to my instincts every time my brain wanted me to run for my life, I would have missed all kinds

(continued)

of opportunities and experiences in life. My brain tried to keep me safe from any sort of conflict, excitement and uncertainty — all a part of life and potential opportunities. So, I had to figure out a way not to let the rising panic of those fight or flight messages dictate my reactions, and instead claw my way back to logic. It was all about making a conscious choice rather than letting emotions choose for me.

Sure, not every person would stand on the rocks of a seal colony — knowing they attract sharks — and choose to go for a surf, but the principle was the same for surfing competitions. My body reacted with the same panic, sending adrenaline coursing through my limbs and 'run' signals screaming through my mind. Performance anxiety triggered the same reactions as real danger.

I would go on to have plenty of fears to face in business too. They might be more abstract, like the fear of failure or of making a fool of myself, but they felt equally debilitating. The same spike of adrenaline gave my hands the shakes and flipped my stomach with nervous anticipation. None of these fears was life threatening but my unruly brain went into the same fight or flight response, often leading to procrastination.

Potential dangers aren't something I think about when taking to popular beaches, but when the breaks are a long way from shore or in stormy conditions, which keep all but the diehards away, those thoughts sneak in. Most people don't face that kind of stress every day, but surfers venture out of their normal habitat every morning, facing the threat of being eaten alive at seven and then being back at their desk job an hour later.

Harnessing these emotions and pushing through the initial involuntary response enabled me to take opportunities other people avoided.

Still, nervous stress nearly got the better of me plenty of times, especially when I burnt the candle at both ends so my endurance and resilience were low, and my ability to make smart decisions was reduced.

Arduous travel schedules between surfing events, such as long-haul flights and overnight drives, were common. A memorable one for me was the drive from Spain back to France. We were all exhausted from the recent travelling and a big day of surfing but needed to return the hire car to the Bordeaux Airport, which required non-stop driving.

We took turns, but it was a struggle. The others saw me pop a couple of pills.

'Hey, what are those?' one friend asked.

'Someone in the US competition recommended them to me. They're some kind of energy pill and they're insane, dude.'

'Give us a look.'

I handed over the packet. 'You can't get them in Australia, but I just bought them over a chemist counter in America.'

'What's in them?'

I shrugged. 'Probably just a high dose of caffeine.'

All I knew was they worked. A bunch of us had taken them one night before a party and ended up staring at the ceiling in the early hours, unable to sleep.

'Cool. Leave them in the console and whoever is driving can pop a couple so they don't fall asleep.'

I was super exhausted, but wired from the pills, and that's when strange things started happening. It was my turn to drive and everyone else was sleeping in various positions of slouching in their seats. Blair was in the front passenger seat and kept leaning forward to stare at me, but when I turned my head to tell him to piss off, he was reclined on his seat, sleeping. Over and over again this happened, frustrating the heck out of me.

Next, I saw a horse and cart up ahead, but as we got closer it disappeared. Great, so I was awake, but also hallucinating. I cracked the window open to breathe the cool, cleansing air.

Passing through a toll booth, I misjudged the gap and hit the gutter, blowing out a tire. This seemed like a good time to rotate drivers — right after we unpacked everything from the back of the car on the side of a dark roadway in the middle of nowhere to change the tire.

We were all haggard with exhaustion when we eventually made it to the Bordeaux Airport and returned the hire car to the assigned parking area. The sun was rising over the airport building as we shouldered our luggage, which felt as though it had been packed with lead. I couldn't wait to check in and sleep the entire way to the Canary Islands.

> **I couldn't wait to check in and sleep the entire way to the Canary Islands.**

'I wonder what's going on,' my mate said.

I followed his pointed finger to where there seemed to be an unusually large number of police checking travellers at the entrance.

The date was 12 September 2001. We had no idea that the day before in New York City two aeroplanes hijacked by terrorists had brought down the Twin Towers and sent airports globally into the highest level of security.

'Oh crap!' I suddenly pictured the realistic-looking plastic gun I'd been carrying at the bottom of my bag since South Africa.

You're a dead man, whispered Bronco. *What kind of idiot carries around a five-dollar plastic gun at an airport? I can just see it now when you pull that thing out for inspection. Best case, you're gonna get tossed in jail. Worst case, the guards think it's real, freak out and shoot you. The end.*

A bead of sweat trickled down my temple as we loitered in the car park. It might have been my imagination, but the security guards seemed to be eyeing us. I let the others go on ahead.

Right before the entrance, the path curved behind a corner of the building, putting me out of sight of the security officers. Without hesitation, I threw my bag to the ground and plunged an arm in, groping around for the toy gun. A couple of other travellers gave me a wary look and a wide birth.

Like a hero in a spy movie, I tossed the magazine full of plastic bullets into a nearby circular metal bin, and the gun into an open sand-filled astray.

Then I rezipped the bag and hurried away from the scene of the crime. I didn't breathe easy until I was on board the next plane, all the while waiting for some poor, shocked tourist to raise the alarm when they spotted a gun by the sidewalk.

◆ ◆ ◆

It was a relief to arrive in the Canary Islands, refreshed by sleep and coming off the back of the win in Pantín, Spain. When I'd arrived in Spain, I'd been down to my last $300 and, after the destruction of my surfboard, I'd been convinced that was the end of the road for me and I would head home after the event. In a strange way, the feeling of having nothing to lose relieved the stress and cleared my head enough for a semi-final finish in the main event and to take out the aerial competition, significantly boosting the bank balance. I now had enough to sustain me through the three events in the Canaries.

I started to feel like the universe had my back when things were down. It was like a new belief that things would always be okay was starting to form. I felt like I performed at my best when my back was against the wall. That's when I stripped things back and all distractions disappeared.

I felt like I performed at my best when my back was against the wall.

Although the Canary Islands are an autonomous community of Spain, they are physically closer to Morocco. The surfing tour visited three of the islands, each like an entirely different world, which made for a unique adventure. Tenerife was a mountainous party island with plenty of tourists and night life; something was always happening. Gran Canaria was formed during volcanic eruptions and its lush mountains made up the bulk of the island centre, with fascinating fossil beaches on the more exposed northern coast. Lanzarote looked like another planet with its exposed volcanic rock, strange and porous with a coating of ultra-fine black dust. The sand on the beach where the surfing competition was held was crushed black rock that was easily stirred up and suspended in the water. It clung to my skin and collected in my board shorts.

Now I was in a different mindset. I felt like things had ended in Spain when I was running out of money, so this all felt like a bonus and didn't have the same pressure. I got on a roll with my surfing and had a semi-final finish in all three events, banking enough money to comfortably allow me to continue onto Japan and Brazil.

I was able to relax and enjoy myself here, although I still had to battle that fight or flight reflex before each competition — convincing my brain there was no immediate danger, and making the most of every opportunity on the waves. I realised I had been carrying a belief that while I could do well in a single event, doing well in multiple events in a row was impossible for me. Once I had a run of good results that belief was gone. In a strange way, just the change in beliefs changed my results.

An internal battle was still going on, though. My mission to make decent money had me torn between going home with the winnings — now close to $10000, which would keep me going for a while at home — or spending it to get to more events and potentially win more money and enjoy the next adventure. I was caught in a constant balancing act between saving money and living a life rich in experiences.

Battling limiting beliefs

Having worked with a sports psychologist on my beliefs around what I could and couldn't accomplish in my surfing career, it became clear that I had a bunch of limiting beliefs. I didn't even realise I had these beliefs till he worked through them with me. The limiting beliefs I had included I didn't deserve to win when I surfed against my heroes, I couldn't bounce back after a good result and back it up with another good result, and I got too nervous and that made me lose. I realised from then on that all my beliefs about what I could

(continued)

and couldn't do were garbage. They were all made up by me, so why couldn't I make up new ones that served me better?

I started to have different thoughts about my future regarding business, which changed everything. I asked myself, 'What if I could make decent money while having an awesome lifestyle and travelling just as much as I have been to surf around the world?' I had previously carried a belief that this wasn't possible—I thought I would have to work 9 am to 5 pm and be tied to a business location. I decided to build businesses that allowed me to surf around the world—and seven years after I made this decision a very experienced business coach told me she believed my business was the only real lifestyle business she had ever seen. I was travelling around six months of each year to surf and explore, while making more money than most business owners she knew. She herself had sold a business for $500 million and mentored a lot of great businesses, so it was a nice acknowledgement.

Lessons from the ocean
Your beliefs about yourself are BS

What beliefs are you holding onto? Do you find yourself thinking things like, I'm not techy, I don't understand social media, I'm too shy (or too old, too young, not experienced enough) to ask? It's likely these kinds of thoughts are just beliefs you've made up about yourself.

We're all consistent with our beliefs, because it's easier to respond to situations consistently based on what we have done in the past, rather than rethinking how we would like to respond to every new situation. That would be too exhausting. If you believe you're not an early riser, for example, and that you can't function early in the morning, you will respond this way every time you consider having an early start. If, as another example, you believe you aren't a technical person, you will respond this way when faced with something technical. And guess what? You will continue to not be an early riser and you will continue to be non-technical, because you don't change the belief and, therefore, don't change your actions.

If you're looking to change some of your beliefs, even just reviewing the belief is a great start. Ask yourself, 'Who made up this belief?'

Working with a cafe owner a few years ago, I realised he had a lot of limiting beliefs about which types of marketing would work for his business. We were working through different strategies to apply, but he kept saying, 'I've tried that, and it doesn't work for my business.'

I've worked with a lot of cafes and restaurants and have had amazing success with many of the strategies he was ruling out. Just because he had had poor results in the past, he assumed they would continue not to work for his industry and would never work. I explained some examples of ways to create free publicity, one of which was a strategy to create a very high-end offering to give the media something to talk about and to create a perception that the business offered very high quality options. This kind of perception usually led to a business selling more of its mid-level-priced offerings.

After a lot of back and forth, he decided to give the strategy a go. We helped him draft a press release to send to the media. He ended up with a story online, and a half-page photo of him with the story in print on one of Australia's biggest media platforms. And his high-end offering? A super expensive toasted sandwich. A funny product, but one that produced epic results. He had his busiest and most profitable week ever after the story was published.

Carve your path

◆ What limiting beliefs are you carrying around? We all have them no matter how great we think we are. Think of an area in life you would like to advance. It could be related to career, business, education, health, a relationship, family, fun or any numbers of things in life.

◆ Have a good think about what you believe about yourself in any area that just came to mind. Write down what comes up for you. Do you think you're good at this aspect of your life? Do you think you have time for it? Do you think you're really capable in it? Now ask yourself—who made up these beliefs?

◆ Now rewrite any changes you would like for your beliefs in these areas. Keep in mind changing beliefs is not as simple as just writing them down; however, you have cracked the shell by simply following this process. You've realised your beliefs are made up by you, so you can make up new ones.

◆ Practise saying the new beliefs to yourself. The more you practise saying these new beliefs—and practising new actions to support the beliefs—the sooner they will become reality. Continuing with the examples from earlier, if your old belief was that you were bad with technology, start playing with technology. If it was that you weren't a morning person, set the alarm for an early start—and stick with it to make it a new normal for you over time.

CHAPTER 11
JAPAN AND BRAZIL
Invest in growth

Descending into Tokyo International Airport was like landing on a helipad in the ocean, with a metropolitan sea stretching all the way to the imposing white cap of Mount Fuji in the distance. By now I was into my seventh year on tour, and riding high on recent magazine and surfing video exposure. A bunch of surfing pictures had even been sent to Japan and used in their magazines as editorial and advertising images. From as soon as I landed, I was treated like royalty in Japan.

An unassuming Japanese man, slim, neatly dressed in surf-branded clothing and with a sparkling smile, picked me up at the airport in a sleek white mini-van to personally deliver me to my accommodation. I struggled to pronounce his name properly, but I mumbled out 'Sheeeshe', which made him smile. I was surprised and thrilled to find he was my personal host for the duration of the event, organised by one of my sponsors. He even had an envelope full of cash to cover our expenses.

He offered me the back seat of the car, but I preferred to sit up front — being ushered from place to place and having my every need attended to was the ultimate 'rockstar treatment'. It felt very decadent — and I loved it!

Sheeeshe told me we were heading to the country, which to me looked very built up with a 7/11 general store every few minutes and busier roads than what I had grown up with.

The accommodation was like a hotel, but our suite had two rooms — one a lounge room and the other an open room for sleeping, with a woven straw floor and roll-out mattresses.

The toll of constant travel, and the uncertainty that came with it, was really starting to weigh on me, so it was a relief to be in a totally different setting with a new crowd of people. Even the company of best mates wore thin after months on tour and I longed for the familiarity of home.

In between the surfing event, my host showed me the local sights and experiences, including unidentifiable (to me) but delicious foods, jostling market places, and a popular karaoke bar where I belted out an off-key rendition of 'Yellow Submarine' by The Beetles. I even tried my hand at Pachinko, which is like a combination of a slot machine and pinball machine. As the player, you control the speed that small metal balls are shot into the machine, with the balls then bouncing around on different paths. If your balls end up on the right path, you win more balls, which get weighed and traded for cash. The sound of hundreds of these machines with metal balls bouncing around inside them was intense.

I also tried visiting a men's sentō (public bath) in the hotel, which was a nerve-wracking experience. It's a place to wash, soak in hot baths or relax in steamy sauna rooms, but with a twist: no bathing suits were required. It was a peaceful haven, but relaxing and socialising naked (as I'd discovered at the French nudist camp) was an entirely foreign concept to me. I was used to life in board shorts.

My initial response was to cover up with the small towel provided, but my host stripped off and sat on a little stool, and then gestured for me to do the same, explaining that washing while standing was rude. At this point, I was the odd one out with clothes still on, so (again using my experience from France) I swallowed the lump in my throat and followed suit. We washed our bodies thoroughly side by side.

After that, we migrated to the communal baths, where I had to tie my longish hair into ponytail to prevent it touching the water, which apparently was also rude. Once I was immersed, I could finally relax and sink into blissful, warm contemplation.

A niggling sense that my surfing career was coming to an end had been plaguing me for a while now. I couldn't be sure whether it was the spate of difficult situations that had led me to battle with Bronco, the stress of fluctuating fortunes and an uncertain future, the repetition of travelling to the same places and not feeling much progress, or just the fact that I'd been away from friends and family for so long, but something was weighing on my mind. When I tried to imagine life after surfing, the vision was fluid and intangible. I didn't have any specific skills that would walk me into a 'normal' career, and my passions were varied.

For my whole life, I'd worked towards surfing success and in many ways I'd had a good run, but what was next? I had friends at home who now had serious jobs. Who would employ me? Did I even want to be employed after a lifetime of shaping my own destiny?

When I tried to imagine life after surfing, the vision was fluid and intangible.

Finding new challenges, and new mentors

I realise now that I needed to learn something new. I needed mental stimulation. Talking to a few of the higher ranked older surfers at the event and seeking some advice, which they gave freely, I realised I needed new mentors, not only in surfing but also in the areas I wanted to go next in life, growing my business ideas. Guidance from mentors and investing in my personal growth had always created a new sense of possibility. I knew I could be very successful in business; I just needed to find the right mentors, people with real world experience, to guide me.

I knew it was important to have a purpose after quitting pro sports because I'd seen many athletes before me lose their way, struggling with substance abuse as they grappled with adapting to a new reality—a new normal without being idolised as you globetrot, doing the thing you love.

Hell, no! If I knew anything, I knew I would go insane. I knew I wasn't wired to be a 'nine to five' kind of person. It just wouldn't work.

My results in Japan were mediocre, triggering a new surge of anxiety. All the insecurities and defeatism returned with a vengeance, and I toyed with the idea of quitting straightaway and heading for home. I'd had a good run being able to compete internationally for seven years and maybe the time had come.

> **I was not a quitter. No matter how difficult things got.**

No. I was not a quitter. No matter how difficult things got, one of my strengths was being able to stay the course and finish what I started. So, I decided to leave Japan early and get to Brazil to prepare for the final event of the year. I had always been learning while competing, but the desire was wearing off and I knew my own business would be my next focus.

After being charged some crazy excess baggage fees while leaving Japan, I was down on cash with no great result in the event there to prop me up.

◆ ◆ ◆

Touching down in Brazil I hoped to reset my mindset and surfing. After an overnight stay in Rio de Janeiro, I packed a surfboard and day bag, and headed out early for the competition site at Barra da Tijuca beach, thirty minutes away. It was good to have time to get my bearings and search for accommodation closer to the event site.

I made myself at home under the shade of an octagonal cafe in the middle of the beach and took in the atmosphere while snacking on an acai bowl. The turquoise water, wide beach and thatched beach huts beckoned me. As luck would have it, I randomly bumped into two Aussie friends, who invited me to stay with them. Accommodation dilemma solved, which was a weight off my shoulders because I was still fatigued from Japan.

The first event didn't yield a good result and I was eliminated early. Watching other surfers getting career best results while I sat around waiting for the next event was pretty painful. I tried to stay positive, I honestly did, but as the saying goes: idle hands are the devil's workshop. With restlessness came Bronco messing with my head.

What's the point of this surfing escapade? Bronco prodded. *Sooner or later, you'll have to leave and get a real job anyway. You're wasting time, and yet here you sit with no qualifications or experience for anything else, just being a beach bum. It feels a lot like your life is kinda over at twenty-six. You could always hope for a dramatic ending before you mess it all up — something that fixes you in the collective mind as an eternal success, like being eaten by a shark or a plane falling out of the sky.*

I've always loved reading rockstar biographies, and have read hundreds of them, but I had no desire to end up dying young like many of them did. But maybe Bronco was right. I'd had a good run and the exciting part of my life was over. Maybe it was my time to step away gracefully.

A short domestic flight took me to the next stop in Brazil of Forianópolis. The island is a surfers' paradise and felt similar to my home on Sydney's Northern Beaches, with a variety of sandy beaches to choose from and consistent swells. Not to mention the crowds weren't as bad as those on the beaches in Rio. The island had a laid-back vibe that felt familiar.

Praia Mole beach, where the competition would be held, is a double arched bay named for the soft, squishy sand that sucks your feet in as you walk. It is bracketed by large rock pools between huge granite boulders at the northern end and a bluff to the south. Exposed to the South Atlantic Ocean, it gets consistent ground swells that create a huge variety of powerful waves depending on the swell direction and a number of other factors.

Despite these positives, things didn't improve during the next event; my body was weary with something akin to jet lag, my mind sluggish and my surfing off. My senses were off, so I wasn't reading the conditions well. My motivation was off, so Bronco had a royal old time screwing with my mind and pushing me into my own thoughts and a state close to depression. I knew I wasn't going to do well in the event, but thought maybe I could surprise myself.

On the beach I smiled to my fellow competitors, while wishing I wasn't there at all.

Unsurprisingly, I had another poor result. The trouble was, I didn't even care at this point. I just felt a bit numb. Succumbing to the idea I'd lost this part of the tour, before I'd even surfed it, wasn't something I'd ever done before. This was bad and I needed to break out of the slump.

I prepared to return home for a few weeks with my tail between my legs, ready to pretend these last few events had never happened. I headed to the airport early, hoping to get an earlier flight than the one I booked. There was a spare seat on a flight out of Forianópolis but I had to overnight in Rio.

A previously purchased — inflexible — ticket from London to Sydney didn't seem like such a good idea now and resulted in me doing an unnecessary lap around the globe in my quest to connect with my original ticket home. Some of my surfing buddies who left Brazil at the same time as me arrived in Sydney two days before me.

◆ ◆ ◆

Suffering home sickness, jet lag and confusion about what the hell I would do with my life after surfing made me ripe for Bronco to dig his teeth in and ratchet up my stress. Keeping busy by surfing and training was the best way to keep Bronco silent, but on a long flight home with nothing but regrets and worries to plague my mind, I hit rock bottom.

The first night home in my own bed, jet lag woke me in the wee hours, so I did the only thing with the power to quell my unease. I hit the surf before dawn. As light crept across the water, I sat on my board, staring at the horizon, not bothered about catching waves, just pondering life. Mentally and physically fatigued as I was, my perspective was skewed.

My skin was almost numb to the touch of water, but not from cold. I felt a strange disconnection between me and the world around me, like my skin wasn't mine, it was just a numb layer.

Nothing really means anything except for the thoughts we give it, so is life real or just a string of random thoughts that creates our state of consciousness? One continuous sequence of thoughts, one after the other, like the eternal surge of the ocean, some waves more intense than others, some with higher peaks or lower dips. Is that how we experience life? Like a dream.

Maybe I had already died and this is just a dream. I might be about to wake, like a Japanese businessman sleeping under his desk, and say I had a really cool dream about being a guy who surfed for a career.

Am I in the future, in a virtual reality game about a guy who lived as a surfer, the whole experience lasting a mere minute, and then I will remove my goggles and be back to the real me?

My body and mind floated there beyond the break.

If I kept floating, all the way into space and didn't stop, what would I find? Some say space ends, but what's past that? If something encapsulates space, then surely there's something past the capsule. Another capsule? What's the point of doing anything if we're just such an insignificant moment in time? A speck in a bigger picture?

Maybe our thoughts were multiplying all the time, splitting off from us like atoms. If I took a risk and died, might I be able to leave that atom behind to mourn my death, while another atom splits off taking my conscious thought with it, moving through time having cheated death? I would have no idea that I left the previous atom, so life would seem like a continuous stream.

My mind was scrambled. This was too much for my tired mind to digest.

All of this self-pity and contemplation might sound like a case of spoilt-brat-syndrome — sure, I got to travel the world making a career out of something I loved — but after years of the tour I

> **I needed to learn something new to grow.**

had come home with hardly any cash to my name, mentally and physically exhausted. I was so down on myself that I became physically sick. My head felt feverish, muscles ached and a headache left me drained of energy. Losing events wasn't unusual and I experienced the same symptoms for a day or two afterwards. The greatest sportspeople of all time spend most of their time losing, the greats don't win every event. I knew all that, but this time the depression lingered. I needed to learn something new to grow. I had plateaued and needed progress to stimulate me.

Understanding the power of the mind

These hard-won lessons during my surfing career taught me valuable life skills that would translate into business success. After years of running different businesses, I transitioned to business mentoring in marketing as one of my main focuses. Over the last decade, I have mentored thousands of business owners around the world through a variety of business mentoring programs. So, I have had the privilege of seeing firsthand how powerful the mind is for everyone, including business owners.

It became clear that each of us has a belief in our own personal self-worth, and this will either elevate or limit us.

(continued)

People tend to find ways to stay close to the level of self-worth they believe they deserve, including income. Sounds crazy, right? But it's true.

Business owners will often spend money or limit their actions without even realising they're doing it, to stay at the level of success they're comfortable with. They convince themselves that they're taking the correct actions, when subconsciously they've chosen actions that are limiting them. So many business owners stagnate without consciously knowing why.

As I work with people and support them to get better results in their business, I provide the required accountability as I guide them to do things that stretch their comfort levels and prevent them from slipping back into old patterns, such as spending money on the wrong things or filling time with unnecessary tasks. We all have a natural inclination to stay within our comfort zones because our subconscious wants us to avoid anything unpleasant, which it misinterprets as danger. But—as you've seen through my battle against Bronco—when we step just a little outside of our comfort zone is when we reap real rewards.

We need mentors to guide us when we're going beyond our comfort zone. In business, I see motivated people shifting their focus all over the place without guidance. They have every intention of being successful, but without a mentor they jump from one idea to the next. It's like they're lost in the forest of possibility, trying to run in ten different directions at once but always returning to the same spot. A mentor with experience will help plough a clear path in one direction.

I've actually seen people get short of breath when they see increased sales flowing into their business because, on some level, it's new and scary. I have advised many people to get out of their own way when they reach new levels of success, and sit in the new state of discomfort. Know that they're in the right place when they are uncomfortable. It takes a little time before they start to get comfortable at a new success level, and until it becomes their new comfort zone. As soon as they drop below or rise above a new level of success, once again they get uncomfortable.

Having a mentor to guide you through these times of discomfort is priceless. You need the reassurance a mentor can provide, and you need someone to give you a different perspective to your own, which will be guided by your own limiting beliefs. Having a clear plan for what to do with increased success or income, before it happens, can help you avoid slipping back into old habits and comfort zones.

This is something I assist my clients to map out early, so when growth happens we can sit back and enjoy the ride without strangling our own progress.

Lessons from the ocean
Invest in growth

If you take one thing away from this book, it should be this: become a lifelong learner. Continue to learn in the areas where you need support the most. If you're a business owner and want to continue to grow your business, you should be a lifelong learner of marketing. I own a marketing company with a team of world-class marketers, but I'm still learning. Every part of business and marketing can always be made better.

In life and business, we either continue to grow in terms of our knowledge and experience, or we plateau while the world around us and everyone in it keeps growing.

I see people worry a lot about spending money on their growth and development, and of course you should do your due diligence. But remember—your knowledge will come with you on any venture for life, so it's a good investment. Wherever possible, learn from people who have done or are doing what you want to achieve.

If you've found the right mentor, coach or community but you're worried about the price, think about how much you value yourself and your own success. You're really investing in yourself, so are you worth it? How much do you value your own goals? We've only got one crack at this life (as far as we know).

Investing in yourself is also motivating—just the fact that you're spending money on yourself means you'll want to see a return, so you'll be more motivated to take action.

I personally want the best for myself, so I'm happy to pay for quality.

Let me give you an example of how powerful seeking advice and a mentor can be. A brewery owner enquired about working with me. He had been running a brewery for just over four years and had invested his life savings into it, even selling his family home to fund it. He knew the business had a lot of potential to grow but he felt stuck, like he had tried everything and was at the point where the business had hit a plateau, and it was make or break. The business hadn't grown at all in the last twelve months and competitors had popped up not far from his brewery, so stress was mounting.

After an initial chat, we decided it would be a great fit for us to work together. I could see some strategies he could implement immediately to get a boost in sales quickly, so I ran him through what to do. We then scheduled our first official mentoring call for a week later. The interesting thing is that by the time the following call came around — only a week later — he had already implemented everything I'd said on the first call. He had also come up with other new ideas and he had his biggest weekend of sales ever. He credited this to our conversation and the ideas we spoke about.

The implementation of marketing strategies in those seven days was more than he had implemented in the entire previous six months. He was over the moon.

I believe his motivation and enthusiasm in those seven days was because of two things: clarity, because he knew what to work on, and focus, because he had invested money and wanted to see a return asap.

Carve your path

- Get a mentor with real-world results in the areas you need support the most. Be hungry and humble when learning from others who have more experience.

- Spend twenty minutes learning every single day. This could be reading a book, article or email newsletter, listening to a podcast, audio book or webinar, or attending a workshop.

- Join a community of like-minded people, so you can brainstorm and learn from others. A huge variety of communities are out there, and many of these are online. You can join for a fee or some are even free. If you do pay a membership fee, at least you know you're in with a group of serious people.

CHAPTER 12
HAWAII AND HOME (AGAIN)
Learn, have fun and maintain health

As Blair and I shuffled towards yet another flight boarding queue, on our way to Hawaii at the start of my eighth year on tour, his mind must've been considering the same topic.

'What are you going to do when you stop surfing?' he asked.

'I'm not sure. It feels like leaving school, hey?'

'I guess. It's cool, though, that we can show up at any popular surfing spot on Earth and know some of the locals.'

'We've put a lot of travel kilometres behind us and had an epic time. Not sure any of it helps in our next career, though.' I sighed with a slight smile, thinking back over some funny memories, as I handed my boarding pass over to the flight attendant. 'What are you going to do?'

'Try to get a job with one of my sponsors as a sales rep.' Blair shrugged. Somehow he was always clear about what he was doing. 'And you?'

'I did a course on website development in my down time and I'm making a few sites for friends. There's a surfboard business I'm kind of in the process of buying into too, but I don't have money, ha ha.'

With no time to gain other qualifications while surfing and travelling so much, a lot of pro surfers were left in a precarious position when their careers ended. Not only were you an adult in the same position most school leavers find themselves in — faced with the frightening prospect of trying to figure out what to do next — but your very reason for existing was ending.

Most of my life, I'd had a clear purpose: train and win at surfing. Confronting a life without that purpose was truly scary.

My earlier life mission had been to make money, but I was feeling like a failure on that front, with very little equity to show for a seven-year career. Money had come in fits and bursts while competing, with sponsorships just enough to cover travel and equipment. I'd had to rely on sporadic prize money to cover living expenses. Following summer around the globe, however, meant travelling in peak season and the additional costs associated with that.

It's not like surfers earned anywhere near the inflated incomes many ball-based sports commanded; a typical win might net $10 000 to $20 000 with a top-tier win around $50 000 to $100 000, and of course the amounts dropped considerably for a placing. The lucky top ten surfers in the world could make enough money over a career to set themselves up for life, financially, but the majority weren't that lucky.

These were the thoughts filling my mind as we arrived in Hawaii.

◆ ◆ ◆

When the sun's shining and surf's up in Hawaii, cameramen line the beaches in their hundreds and surfers from all around the world line the often-giant waves. The local surfers are giants too, and very protective of their breaks. With so many surfers in the water, there were never enough waves for everyone, so the locals dominated, sticking together to ensure they got the lion's share of rides each day.

Every so often, disrespectful visitors got their heads punched in by some mighty big guys, leaving the beach with bloody faces and broken boards. I was never the focus of any aggression in Hawaii, but I made sure to respect the locals' wave priority. After all, the same rule applied everywhere.

Localism in the surf was nothing new to me. It existed in my hometown of Narrabeen too. I had my moments too, often taking more waves than surfers I didn't recognise at my home break. I wasn't trying to be nasty; it's just that sometimes with not enough waves for everyone, a natural pecking order prevailed.

Hawaiian waves are renowned for being dangerous. They are bigger than most and break over shallow volcanic reef, which sometimes leads to rash decisions and accidents. When you were desperate to catch a wave, you had to take any opportunity that came your way, often meaning you were not in the perfect spot to catch the wave but went for it anyway.

A couple of my friends over the years hit their heads on the rocky bottom and were knocked unconscious underwater. Luckily, on both occasions, friends noticed a few waves had passed without them surfacing, and rushed in to find them. Their bodies were raised from the depths within minutes, not breathing, and dragged to shore. Being able to clear their airways and get them to the emergency services saved their lives.

Many surfers were not so lucky, as the long list of surfers who met an unfortunate end attests to. The waves don't discriminate between big names, locals and tourists.

Being impatient on the waves in Hawaii is a good way to get your arse kicked by the power of the ocean, and I learnt a lot of valuable lessons about fortitude and tolerance facing mammoth walls of water that can't be controlled.

◆ ◆ ◆

The first time I'd landed in Hawaii, Keenan and I had been inexperienced travellers with little support, having to find our own way around and sleeping on the beach in lieu of the first night's accommodation.

This time a carload of other surfers and I were met at the airport by the beaming Australian Billabong Team Manager, Sam. We piled into a rental van and were driven across the lush island and past the now dark pineapple fields.

> **I learnt a lot of valuable lessons about fortitude and tolerance facing mammoth walls of water.**

As we approached the North Shore, eager to be back on the strip of coast with some of the most amazing surf on the planet, a car sped past at lightning speed.

'Geez, I'm doing the speed limit. I guess they're in a hurry,' mumbled Sam as he glanced at the dashboard.

The large silver sedan disappeared around the bend ahead. Moments later, our van rounded the same corner, and I was surprised to see a long, straight, empty road ahead.

'Where the hell did that car go?' I said to no-one in particular. It was fast, but not that fast. Everyone in the van peered through the front windscreen, brows furrowed.

The team manager shrugged. 'Must have pulled into a driveway.'

That fast? I guessed so.

'Hang on!' yelled Dan, one of the fellow Billabong team riders, pointing to the roadside.

'I saw it too,' I said. 'Taillights. Sideways. We better go back,' I blurted out as my mind wondered what we were about to see.

Sam braked quickly and turned around the van. We were all silent as we collectively held our breaths.

'There,' I called.

Sure enough, the large silver sedan was balancing on its side vertically. Steam, or maybe smoke, billowed from under the crumpled front end of the car that rested against a heavy stone wall that separated a bike path from the road as it ran along the strip of beaches on Oahu's North Shore.

'Shit!' Everyone in the van said simultaneously.

Doors were flung open, and we rushed towards the wreck.

My muscles were tensed as nerves took hold of me, heart beating at a million miles an hour, gasping shallow breaths. This was bad.

Dark fluid leaked from the exposed undercarriage, one wheel had been bent sideways and smoke curled from what was left of the front of the car. As I rounded the vehicle, the damage looked so much worse. The windscreen was shattered but holding together in a misshapen sheet.

Tiny flames dripped inside the torn apart front end.

'It's gonna blow!' Sam yelled, leaping back.

We all ran twenty feet away from the wreck and crouched close to the ground.

After a couple of minutes, I stood. 'Maybe it's not going to blow,'

'There are flames,' Dan reiterated. 'It might go any second.'

Uncertain glances were passed around like a game of whispers, becoming more urgent with each passing. It was after midnight in an area with very few lights.

'I'll go for help,' Dan volunteered. 'I saw a house just through those trees.'

Other surfers took off running with him.

'I'm going to try to get the people out,' I announced. I rounded the car again, dreading what I'd find inside. I ran to the windscreen and got right up close to see if we could assist anyone stuck in the car. I peered through a hole where the windscreen gaped away from the metal frame.

'Ohhh, god,' I mumbled. 'Only the driver,' I called out louder so others could hear. 'But it doesn't look good.'

'Who's in there?' someone yelled toward me. I tried to speak but choked up, turning my head and retching the contents of my stomach onto the grass. There was no getting him out ourselves and I could tell he was dead. He looked completely broken.

Through the thundering of my pulse over my eardrums I heard someone yelling.

'They've called an ambulance. Someone will be here soon.'

A few locals in various states of undress and night attire hurried towards the wreck. One moved people back to a safe distance.

And then we heard a gut-wrenching cry as a burly bloke in board shorts ran for the car.

'Nooo! Fuck no, it's Sal.' The man dropped to his knees beside the wreck and released a guttural roar into the night sky.

It was so utterly shattering to watch that everyone froze. Welcome to paradise.

We stayed until the emergency services arrived, and then continued to our accommodation in solemn silence, each person alone with their own morbid thoughts. The memory of that night was forever scarred into my mind and I would lie awake at night for many weeks, reliving the horror.

Reordering priorities

Being confronted by death like that got me thinking about how precious and fragile life is. Why would I care what anyone thought of me? If I died right this minute, what would I regret? I wouldn't regret not winning one more competition or bringing home more prize money. I would regret not trying my hardest. I would regret being distracted. I knew I needed to focus and *just catch the two best waves*.

These thoughts juggled my priorities into a new order and prepared me for a new chapter of my life. I now felt a sense of urgency. I believed I was unemployable in a standard business, but I also knew I needed to work on something that allowed me to surf every day. That was non-negotiable. Without realising it at the time, I had begun to reverse-engineer my future career to fit with my lifestyle first.

I returned home after a month of surfing and decided to reduce my surfing commitments to part-time in favour of new projects. I bought into a surfboard manufacturing business and supported my income with web development services. Having no employment that provided a regular income, I'd initially asked my father for a loan to buy into the surfboard business. He couldn't provide a loan at that moment, but offered me the advice to ask the bank for a $20 000 loan and say it was for white goods — according to Dad, the banks seemed to approve loans for white goods more easily than other loans. I gave it a shot and got the loan. I was in business!

I stepped into the surfboard business and quickly realised I preferred website development. Manufacturing was fun and I would be a part of that business for five years, but something about the internet clicked within my brain. Developing the most efficient pathway for potential customers to be directed to the information they wanted — and that a business owner needed them to find — was obvious to me in a way it didn't seem to be for others. The part of the process that excited me the most was how to make websites more visible to potential customers and, therefore, generate more sales. This was when my real passion for online marketing developed.

I threw myself into this new purpose, learning everything I could about internet marketing, travelling to conferences around the world and testing techniques in real time.

Within a short time, I was able to create a few small online businesses that generated revenue. First, I set up a surf coaching website that was fully automated and generated cash for me. Then I used the same repeatable process to set up a few websites that sold people fully automated language courses in French, German and Spanish. I realised I could recruit people from anywhere on Earth to assist with just about anything I needed online.

My sites were getting great results through my internet marketing efforts and word spread fast. Within twelve months I was being invited to present my knowledge at events hosted by private colleges and universities.

Within a few short years, the decision to focus on internet marketing would lead me to create a business that made more money per week, often in a single day, than I did in most full years of my surfing career. In my mind, each challenge was — and is — a surfing event. I still approach bigger business events with the same routine I used for surfing events, including a warm-up surf the morning of and healthy eating routines. I found internet marketing allowed me to see wins as clearly as I did in competitive surfing. Marketing and sales have clear outcomes, and measurable wins.

I'm still learning, applying and assisting others with internet marketing, and have now for over twenty years. I developed a workshop to help train small business owners to grow their business and, again, I approach these workshops like a surfing event. I run the same workshop over and over, year after year, perfecting every word in the two-hour session.

In the workshop industry, people believe they must continually offer different workshops on different topics to keep people coming back; however, I do the opposite. I knew if I created the greatest marketing workshop on Earth, people would keep coming back and would comfortably refer their friends. Indeed, people would love the workshop so much that they would want to continue working with me. The workshop developed my reputation and, as a business, we started running it in over twenty cities globally and online. I tried to simply be the best in the space.

The workshop has generated more than $30 million in sales for my business. I also continue to oversee hundreds of millions in my clients' businesses — and, in my mind, all I'm doing is surfing. See the simple thing that works and go after it. Just catch two good waves.

For years on the pro surfing circuit, I'd been acutely aware of the need to be a marketing tool for my sponsors' brands, and in business the same principles apply. The more exposure I could generate, the more widely my brands were recognised and the faster revenue increased. Marketing was a sought-after skill and I enjoyed doing it.

> **See the simple thing that works and go after it. Just catch two good waves.**

I honed so many mindset strategies during my surfing career, and I've now harnessed these in business. These include a drive to compete and see results; approaching challenges by getting into competition mode, so I was pumped with excitement but focused and in control; and being able to keep my cool in order to navigate challenging situations.

The triggers and emotions associated with anxiety were my familiar friends and, when I felt them flowing through my body, I was able to recognise and take control of them. I no longer tried to ignore this part of me; instead, I harnessed the energy and redirected it towards getting tasks done that would move my business towards its goals.

As I've already mentioned, I love reading rockstar biographies. I love to see how people with incredible talent go from nothing to living larger than life existences. Then, the outlining of the rapid climb to fame and riches when they are successful, and the excess and overwhelm that comes with many of the rockstar stories is so intriguing. These experiences are similar to the feelings of discomfort we all feel when we reach new levels of success.

Progressing through the stages of business

The hindsight of having worked with thousands of business owners over the years provides me with the clarity to see that they move through routine stages in a similar way athletes move through the surfing world tour rankings.

Business owners start off overflowing with optimism, eager to create the business of their dreams, excited about seeing it come to fruition through choosing and registering a business name, designing a logo, building the brand assets and figuring out what product or service they'll deliver. It's as exciting as having your feet sink into warm, gritty sand as you stare across sparkling water, centring yourself — taking in everything you feel, smell and hear — when you're preparing for your first year of competing full-time and going to new places.

After they get their business set up and have been operating for a little while, business owners start to notice that money is going out but not a whole lot is coming in. The realisation of how challenging business ownership can be hits them between the eyes. And they start to panic.

Most won't make it through these early challenges. Those who do survive don't realise more crisis points are still ahead of them. Just like with surfing, the reality soon sinks in that no matter how talented they are, they will spend the majority of their time losing. No-one wins every time! Then they lift their gaze to see that they're surrounded by many other excellent surfers (or businesses). They are just one of many.

(continued)

These crises can drag business owners down into the depths of self-doubt, causing them to seriously consider throwing in the towel or parking the idea for later. Others will come up with new ideas, believing this is the solution, when really it is only a distraction from the challenges they *need to face*. No matter how many fabulous new ideas they come up with and how many different angles they come at the idea from during the exciting start-up phase, they will never succeed unless they can face the challenges head-on and push through to the other side.

Only the most dedicated business owners — those who stick to their goals, don't shy away from difficult situations and battle through those crisis points — will start to experience success.

This doesn't mean it will then be all smooth sailing. Far from it. Challenging situations will always arise, such as a key employee leaving with only a moment's notice, or a landlord kicking you out of the perfect office space, or you sparing no expense on an office fit-out right before sales come to a grinding halt. Even situations you wouldn't think could push you outside of your comfort zone can.

I remember being short of breath when huge amounts of money first started flowing into the business bank account. I'd never experienced anything like it. Was I worthy of this kind of success? Would it last? Just breathe, Christo, and *catch two more waves*. Focus on the triggers that brought the money in, not the money itself. Money is an outcome of the key actions.

Through the sheer will of never giving up, continuing to do the hard tasks and maintaining success for a long period, business owners usually make decent money.

It makes me smile when I look back on my journey — that overnight success I was chasing sure took a long time and continues to be a whole lot of hard work. Something I've found to be true of many successful people is that they are humble because they understand the sacrifices required to get there. On the other hand, people who purport to know it all and have the answer to everything tend to be those who haven't yet accomplished much.

And after sustaining success for a long time, it's natural to start to look for the next thing to challenge the mind and fulfil a higher purpose. This often comes in the shape of a passion project, charity work or mentoring others. Giving their time to support up-and-coming or disadvantaged newbies is a common theme among professional athletes.

To maintain motivation through all stages of business and in life in general, we must continually be learning to stay mentally stimulated, having fun and looking after our health. Letting any of these three areas slip is just not sustainable.

These rock stars often go from playing songs in their bedroom to suddenly being a household name, in the glare of media scrutiny with everyone wanting a piece of them. Many turn to substance abuse to cope with the emotional roller-coaster. But it's their personal processes that captivate me the most. The way they create, letting the noise of fame and everything going on around them fall away so they can focus on what they need to do, can be fascinating.

Often, they try to get back to sitting alone in a bedroom making music, not worrying that their lyrics and rhythms will be blasted to millions of fans later on.

It doesn't matter how successful they are, everyone has their own version of Bronco to battle — that little subconscious voice telling you you're not good enough, fast enough, strong enough, smart enough. Telling you it's too risky or too much trouble. Steering you away from challenges and into more comfortable situations. Situations that feel familiar, but have little chance of propelling you to your next success, because now we know that success only comes from pushing through discomfort and operating outside of your comfort zone.

I often hear business owners say things like, 'I know I need to work with you to grow my business, I just don't feel ready.'

Focus on the process, not the result.

The truth is, in business, we are constantly growing and trying to reach the next level. Therefore, we *never actually feel ready for it, or feel fully satisfied for long when we have it*. Growth feels uncomfortable and staying stagnant feels deflating. So it's at the edge of discomfort where success lies.

We need to experience discomfort to grow.

It's not about working longer hours or harder; all that matters are results, not the hours you put in. It all comes back to Nick's simple advice: 'Just catch two good waves, Christo.' Focus on the process, not the result.

To win a surfing competition, I needed to tune out all the noise and other competitors around me and focus my attention on the feel of the water slipping across my body, connecting me to the ocean, and then on turning the board into the right part of the wave at the right time.

It's the same in business. You need to concentrate on the processes that deliver results, rather than worry about all the sensational hype in the market or what anyone might be saying about you. Just be present in the moment. By focusing on the simplicity of what you're doing, like the feel of wax on a surfboard or water on your skin, you will complete the task. Results will follow.

Keep chipping away at those high-impact tasks that bring in the biggest returns, and be relentless in doing more and more of those tasks every week; *no matter what's going on around you.*

Let me give you an example of not being thrown off centre. Out of the blue one day, my accountant called me. 'Are you sitting down?'

Strange thing to ask. 'Yeah, what's up?'

'Have you got money in the business account?'

We both knew full well he could see the balance via our accounting software, so what on Earth was he getting at? My belly roiled with dread as a hundred horrible scenarios ran through my mind. Maybe we'd been hacked and lost all our money, or something equally terrible.

I took a deep breath and braced for his news.

'There should be a little bit in the bank,' I said. 'Why?'

'You've got a *big* tax bill.'

'How big?' I murmured.

'Mid six figures. I know you've paid a lot of tax already, but you also had a large profit, so this is a big one.'

My jaw was slack with stunned silence.

'Are you going to be okay?' he checked.

I like to use money when it's available. I'm not the kind of person to leave cash sitting in the bank, so every cent I'd earned was moved somewhere to investments or spent. My accountant knew I didn't have a lot of cash just sitting around waiting for the tax office to swoop in and grab it.

'Probably not enough in the bank right now.' A nervous giggle slipped out and my intestines coiled tight like a death adder retreating to protect itself. 'I've spent a lot. Bought the shop and apartment next to my office and renovated it too.'

As if you won't be able to pay the tax bill, Bronco scoffed in a rare supportive tone.

Years ago, I used to think Bronco implied that I was no good at what I did. I've since learnt he merely enforces my own expectations. If I'm not doing something to the best of my ability, Bronco lets me know — in no uncertain terms. He lets me know if I'm wasting my time, or should stop being lazy, or should do things to a better standard. This helps me perform at my optimal level.

I have now embraced Bronco as a permanent part of my psyche. He became proficient at limiting how far I could go during my surfing career, but I understand him better now. Sure, he still works hard to limit my business success at every opportunity, especially when I'm reaching for a new goal or implementing something new, but I now know how to work with him.

If Bronco gives me the slightest indication that something isn't good enough, then I know I need to keep at it until he has been silenced. So, Bronco scoffing at the challenge of paying the tax bill brought a sense of calm determination to me.

'Yeah, it will be all good,' I told the accountant confidently. 'I'll work it out.'

Fuelled with the extra motivation from Bronco, I stayed focused on those high-impact tasks to keep riding the wave of growth my business was experiencing and managed to pay the tax bill. Lesson learnt, though, and I made sure we had a process in place to plan for future large tax bills.

In my head, Bronco occasionally takes on the voice of someone I look up to. He chastises me in the voice of that person, telling me what I *should* be doing. So, I sometimes advise customers to imagine what someone they admire would do in challenging situations. This changes the tone of their own subconscious to make it a more positive voice to guide them.

I've also found another way to control Bronco and change his focus very quickly. In times when I want to perform creatively and feel like I'm on the top of my game, I internally change Bronco's name to 'Jim'—Jim after Jim Morrison, lead singer of The Doors, and Jim after Jimi Hendrix, the greatest guitar player to ever live. Both of these Jims were extremely creative and

> I feel creative, interesting and have nothing to prove. That helps me freely dance in the surf and in business.

lived short but impactful lives. For me, they're intriguing characters, who I have read a lot about. 'Let's do this, Jim,' I tell myself and my whole state instantly changes — I feel creative, interesting and have nothing to prove. That helps me freely dance in the surf and in business.

Mentors have also been hugely important to me. I have always learnt from people who had already achieved the success I was chasing, by watching them, listening to their lessons learnt, and paying for coaches and specialists. This was a no-brainer in the pro-surfing world, so it made sense for the business world too.

These mentors helped hold me to a high standard and to stay the course when discomfort threatened to derail me.

I deliberately identified areas in my business where I could benefit from someone else's experience, and then sought out the best in that field—such as the best in the world at YouTube ads, or a woman who sold her business for $500 million. If you're at a certain level in business and feel dissatisfied with your progress to the next level, and are pushing against personal resistance, then ideally you should hang around people (which might include paying for mentoring) who are capable of influencing you in a positive way.

And to this day I still dedicate twenty minutes a day to gaining new knowledge. None of this knowledge is ever wasted. It either builds my world view or is applied to my business, and often gets shared with my customers through business advisory sessions.

Lessons from the ocean
Learn, have fun and maintain health

Most small businesses fail. That's a reality. It's a real shame but, no matter what, some ideas just won't take off, and often business owners and high achievers get burnt out. Trying to do too much in one area of life creates an imbalance, and leaves you unable to cope when the inevitable hard times come—no matter how successful you are.

I often hear excuses from business owners on why they can't focus on their wellbeing—excuses like, 'Once my business gets to a certain level, then I'll adjust my lifestyle to look after my health', or 'When I hit $10 million in turnover, I'll take a break'. In my experience, with so many businesspeople it just doesn't work this way. You obviously can work harder to get more done, but you need to have boundaries to maintain momentum. You need to know that a happy you needs to be looked after. If you overwork yourself and neglect your health and happiness, you will burn out. You're the most valuable resource in your business, so you need to be nurtured.

Often I see business owners allowing a better lifestyle for their employees than they do for themselves. The reality is if you don't look after yourself, your employees won't have a job anyway.

As an example of this, I once worked with a lawyer who was working from sunup to sundown, seven days per week while trying to juggle her family life. When she started with me, her two employees were starting work at 9 am and having a one-hour lunch break, often using this to go for a walk or the gym, before having lunch at their desk and then finishing work at 5 pm. The employees had a good balanced day of work and health, with time to play before and after work; however, the business owner was far from it. She was close to a total meltdown when she started with me, stressing about working more to pay for her team members' wages. We worked through marketing systems and then moved these systems to her employees to implement. We also moved more of the lower level work she was doing herself to her employees, and implemented strict boundaries for her to have time for health and family. Only four months later, she was making more money than ever before, working five days and finishing work every day at 5 pm to spend time with family or do exercise. Most importantly, she was happier.

Before working with me and my team, she had been too busy to see what needed to happen to even grow her business. She couldn't get her head above water to see what needed to be done. There's a ceiling on what you can do with your time every day and she had hit it, so she didn't have any space to implement new things. We freed up her time and now she works on higher level, higher paid work, and has time to implement new growth strategies *and* look after herself.

To be fulfilled in business and life, you must continually learn new things, have fun and maintain your health.

Carve your path

- Write down the following three headings in your notebook or tablet: Learn, Fun and Health.

- Add some ideas under each heading of things you would like to do for each of them this week. Keep these ideas simple, so they're achievable. Know that for a happier you at the end of the week, you need to get these things done. You are the most powerful resource in your life to generate success, so make sure you do these to look after yourself and keep success sustainable.

My list will look something like this:

- Learn
  Read business books for 20 minutes per day. Have a chat with a mentor/colleague in business about current goals/challenges.

- Fun
  Go surfing every day for at least 30 minutes and have a dinner out with my partner, or with my partner and friends.

- Health
  Do yoga at least twice a week.

GOING BEYOND THE BREAK

Recently I was sitting with my best mate, Ian, planning a surfing holiday to Indonesia, and I opened my digital calendar to find corresponding free time.

'*What the?*' said Ian as he peered over my shoulder. 'That is not the calendar of a normal human.'

'What do you mean?' I laughed, fairly sure I was in fact a relatively normal human.

'Look at all the stuff you've got going on!'

He pointed as I scrolled down to reveal the rest of the month, ablaze with colour-coded events and actions. And I'd been just as busy in the previous months. In the last two months, I had been to the Maldives twice, and also visited California, Bali and seven cities around Australia to facilitate workshops and business mentoring. I didn't have a single week without flights. *Hmm, maybe he had a point.*

'How do you find time to surf? You're like a satellite orbiting the Earth.' He sounded appalled.

'I surf five days a week most weeks. It's an ongoing balancing act.'

I'm still always trying to make my business better as well as find more time to surf. A bunch of things will always be pulling me in different directions, but without surfing in my life I know I won't stay sane.

Keeping busy and feeling productive helps to keep Bronco at bay, but I've found I need to balance that productivity with rejuvenation. As I've mentioned, doing something fun each week, such as surfing or catching up with friends, silences Bronco *and* gives me a sense of wellbeing. I also love learning something new each week to expand my mind and grow my knowledge base.

If I do something in each of my three vital areas each week — grow my business, nurture my health and expand my mind — then I feel good about life.

If I start feeling flat and Bronco turns into a pest, dragging me down into dejection, it's usually because I haven't focused on one of these three areas for a while. When I assess my calendar, I'll find my time has weighed too heavily in one area at the detriment of the others. It's too tempting when running a business to spend all your time picking away at the endless to-do list, while neglecting your health and personal growth.

When I feel like this, it's a sure sign that it's time to catch up with friends for drinks and conversation, go up the coast to surf somewhere different, or maybe challenge my mind by reading a book on a new topic. It's all a part of the continuous mix to stay happy: learn, fun and health.

◆ ◆ ◆

In some ways, not much has changed since I was a scrawny ten-year-old lad racing down to the beach to watch the big boys compete. When the world tour recently came to my home beach of Narrabeen, I was so excited I sat on the beach from dawn until dusk every day of the four-day competition. The thrill of anxiety and excitement that used to course through my veins when I competed still charged through me as I watched others compete. I read the conditions, searched for the best waves and willed them to do well.

One morning I slept in, waking just ten minutes before the first event started. Not wanting to miss a moment of the competition, I threw on clothes and ran out of the house so fast that I forgot to brush my teeth. I didn't leave the beach for ten and a half hours, dragging myself home at 5.30 pm, still wearing my pyjamas under my jeans and jacket.

Things may seem to have come full circle — although I now get a little sore from sitting on the beach all day, without even a milk crate to my name — but I've travelled a very long way to get here.

I hope you've enjoyed the stories of my travels, and gained some insights along the way. I'd love to hear any feedback, as well as any stories of your own successes or wipe-outs — in the surf, in business or in life. (A positive review for this book would also be amazing. I will send you waves of gratitude in return!)

You can get in touch via the following:

- Join me for a free marketing workshop via www.basicbananas.com.
- Get in touch for mentoring or to say hi via support@basicbananas.com.
- Connect with me personally on LinkedIn, Facebook and Instagram – be sure to let me know you read the book.
- Simply say hi if you see me in the surf.

Printed and bound by CPI Group (UK) Ltd, Croydon, CR0 4YY

07/08/2024

14537704-0001